Bicycle
Touring and Camping

Bicycle Touring

By
Edward F. Dolan, Jr.

and Camping

Photographs by Jay Irving

INTRODUCTION BY
AMERICAN YOUTH HOSTELS, INC.

Julian Messner
New York

JULIAN MESSNER and colophon are trademarks of
Simon & Schuster, registered in the U.S. Patent
and Trademark Office.

Design by Irving Perkins Associates

Manufactured in the United States of America.

Library of Congress Cataloging in Publication Data
Dolan, Edward F., 1924–
Bicycle touring and camping.
Bibliography: p.
Includes index.
Summary: A guide to planning, preparing for,
and carrying out short and overnight bicycle
trips.
1. Bicycle touring—Juvenile literature.
2 Camping—Juvenile literature. [1. Bicycle
touring. 2. Camping. 3. Bicycles and bicycling]
I. Irving, Jay, ill. II. Title.
GV1044.D64   796.6   81–21962
ISBN 0–671–42876–4

31032

For Natlee Kenoyer
Good friend

Contents

Introduction

THIS BOOK WAS
written to help you plan short bicycle tours in and
around your home town. Whether you have two hours,
two days, or two weeks, no time is too short for explor-
ing, and cycling can give you the satisfaction of traveling under your own steam. It also provides the chance
to be alone with yourself. Your mind is free to wander,
and your soul to breathe. On your cycle, life surrounds
you; yet you are free to be an observer "just passing
through" or to stop and get involved, as you choose.

For those who prefer touring and camping with
other people, the experience can add new dimensions
to the meaning of friendship. As time passes on the
road or around the campfire, life seems to return to a

simplicity seldom found in "modern" life. And as the challenges, and even the hardships, of the outdoors are met, together, with bare hands and resourcefulness, a sense of confidence is developed in each other and in man's ability to survive.

And so, good luck—and much good fun—to you as you begin your adventures in touring and camping.

Stacy Landau
Public Relations Director
American Youth Hostels
Metropolitan New York Council, Inc.

Bicycle
Touring and Camping

CHAPTER 1

You and Your Bike

YOU HOP ABOARD your bike and pedal off.

Perhaps you plan to ride just a couple of hours and enjoy the countryside near your home. Perhaps you're going to be away all day, with a stop for lunch and a swim at a nearby county or state park. Perhaps you're off with your family or friends for a week-long run that will see you camping out at night or bedding down in a motel or hostel.

Or perhaps you're really ambitious and have in mind a trip across your state—or clear across the country.

Whatever your plans may be as you pedal off,

you've become part of the sport called bicycle touring. Some people believe that a bike trip has to be a
long one to be called a tour. Nothing could be further
from the truth. It doesn't matter whether you plan to
be gone for just a few hours or for weeks. You're
going somewhere, and so you're on tour. And, on
tour, you're in for all sorts of fun.

Bicycle touring can't help being fun. Pedaling
along, you're not locked inside a car. The wind is
brushing your face and you're soaking up all the
fresh air you could wish for. You're riding along silently, and you can hear something other than the
roar of an engine; you can actually hear the birds
singing or a cow mooing over in a pasture. Nor are
you speeding along so fast that everything passes in a
blur; you have the time to see and enjoy the surrounding landscape. Very soon, you begin to feel that
you're a part of the nature that's all around you.

And there's more to the fun. You're getting some
of the greatest exercise in the world as you work
those pedals. And you're facing the fun of one challenge after another. You put yourself to a test every
time you climb a hill to reach your goal for the day—
your destination. You can't help feeling good, and
proud, when you pass all these tests.

The fun of touring has made it one of today's
most popular sports. No one knows for certain exactly
how many Americans are trying their hand at anything from day-long to vacation-long jaunts, but they
must number in the millions. For proof, just look at

the number of bicycles in the United States. They total more than 105 million.

Though the exact number of tourers isn't known, one thing for certain can be said about them: they're people of all ages. Two of the most enthusiastic travelers I've ever met are a husband and wife in their seventies. I know of bicycle clubs that sponsor tours for very young children; the youngsters are usually six and older, but all the clubs ask is that the kids be tall enough to pedal efficiently and safely. And I know of a two-year-old who has become a touring veteran. He's too small to pedal, of course, but he rides happily for miles in a basket seat attached just behind the saddle of his father's bike.

Indeed, touring is fun. If it weren't, it wouldn't attract so many fans of all ages. But, like any other sport, touring is also a demanding pastime. There's much more to it than jumping on your bike and saying, "Let's go somewhere."

For instance, even the shortest jaunt needs to be planned if it's to be really successful. You need to know how to handle your bike correctly if you're to travel for miles without becoming overly tired. You need to know the rules of safe riding. You need to know what to take with you and how best to pack it aboard your bike. And you need . . . well, as you'll see in the next chapters, the list is a pretty long one.

The things that you must know only add to the fun of touring. Many of them, such as the rules of safe riding, will also contribute to the pleasure of your everyday riding near home. And that's the purpose of this book: to talk about all the things that will help to make you an expert tourer and a top-notch daily cyclist.

Shall we get to work? The best way to start is not to grab a map and look for a place to go. It's best to look first at a few facts about you and that lightweight piece of equipment that makes your tours possible—your bike.

A BIKE FOR TOURING

New cyclists always have one question: "What sort of bike will I need for touring?"

Let's answer the question by first saying that your beginning tours should be short ones. You should plan to reach your destination and return home in just a few hours. Pedaling along for miles requires plenty of strength and stamina. Short runs will give you the chance to condition yourself and develop your bike-handling skills. Then you'll be in the best shape possible when it's time for longer trips.

For your first brief outings, your present bike will be just fine. If you happen to own a ten-speed bike, you're really in business. It's the best you can have for any kind of touring (though you can go to a fifteen-speed if you wish). It provides you with those ten great gears. They make it easy for you to travel over all sorts of terrain.

Above, the Schwinn Voyageur SP; *below*, the Schwinn Super LeTour. (PHOTOS COURTESY SCHWINN SALES, INC.)

But suppose that you now own a one-speed or a three-speed bike. Great! You're in business, too. Either one will serve nicely on short trips. When you reach the point where you want to pedal all day long or for days on end, however, you'll really need a ten-speed. There's nothing like it for extended runs.

If you don't own a ten-speed at present, try to keep your mouth from watering for one. Just remember that it can be a pretty expensive piece of equipment. Purchased new, a ten-speed can range from around $200 up to over $3,000. Even secondhand, it can cost a fair-sized bundle. So, unless you have the money, don't be impatient. Stick to your trusty old one- or three-speed while you build your strength and gather touring experience (you're especially lucky if you have a three-speed—or, better yet, a five-speed—because its few gears will do much to make pedaling easier). Enjoy your present bike while you save for a ten-speed. Then head for the bike shop when the right time comes.

DOES YOUR BIKE FIT YOU?

Size is quite as important as the kind of bike you first use for touring. For a comfortable ride, you need a bike that fits your size, whether it's an old one-speed Jake or a brand-new ten-speed Slick.

If the bike is too big or too small for you, you're going to tire quickly and develop some aches and pains in an assortment of muscles that you didn't know you had. Look what happens when the bike is too small. There you are, pedaling along with your knees sticking out to the sides like a couple of jug handles. They're bound to start hurting sooner or later—usually sooner.

And what happens if the bike is too big? Your foot leaves the pedal at the bottom of each down-stroke. You're forced to shift from side to side to keep in touch with the pedals. Very, very soon—(you guessed it!) a sore bottom. Also, if the pedals are too far away at the bottom of the downstrokes, you won't be in full control of the bike. That can be disastrous.

If you're a boy, there's an easy way to see if your bike is a good fit. As shown in the illustration, just stand straddling the bike, with your legs on either side of the top tube. If there is about an inch of space between the tube and your crotch, the bike is basically the right size for you.

It's more difficult for girls to make this measurement because their bikes come without the top tube. But go ahead and try anyway. Just imagine where the top tube would be. Do you seem to have an inch or so of clearance? Good.

If you own a ten-speed, there's yet another way to check for proper size. Have a friend hold the bike upright while you sit on it. Lean forward and grasp the hooks. (Ten-speeds usually have handlebars shaped like rams' horns, and the hooks are the lower sweeps of the horns, down where the handle grips

CHECKING FOR FIT OF TEN-SPEED BIKE

are.) You should be able to hold the hooks with your elbows slightly flexed, just short of being locked. Your backbone should be straight, and your bottom should rest comfortably on the saddle.

These tests should be made on your present bike and should certainly be made when you've got your eye on a new bike. You should never buy a bike that doesn't pass them or that doesn't feel comfortable to you, no matter how fancy and shiny it may be. *Comfortable* is the word you want to remember when making your purchase. If the bike feels comfortable after you've pedaled it around a bit (and always insist that the bike shop let you take a test run before buying), then it's for you. If not, keep on looking.

What if your present bike fails to pass the tests? Don't give up and start looking for a new sport. The chances are that a few minor adjustments in the seat and handlebar heights will make things right. In fact, even if your bike fits, you may want to make these adjustments for riding comfort.

Let's look at them now.

RIDING IN COMFORT

Proper seat height is all-important to comfortable cycling. Quite as important, it helps you to keep the bike under full control and enables you to pump steadily and strongly. The seat should be set at a height that permits your leg to be almost fully extended at the bottom of each downstroke. At that moment, your knee should be just slightly bent. The ball of your foot should touch the pedal at all times.

If your saddle is now at the wrong height, you can easily adjust it. Crouch down and look at the metal post on which the saddle is perched. The post disappears into the body of the bike—actually, into what is known as the seat tube—and is held firmly in place by a clampnut. All that you need do is loosen that clampnut with a crescent wrench. The post will

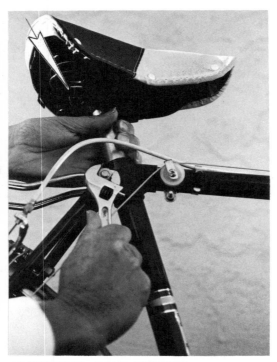

ADJUSTING SEAT HEIGHT

then slide up and down. Experiment with several heights, finally picking the one that seems right. Tighten the clampnut securely between each experiment and after you've made your final selection.

One caution, please: if you raise the seat, be sure to leave at least two inches of the post inside the seat tube. If raised too high, the post could jiggle loose during a ride and come out of the tube. And there you'd be, plunked down on the frame. That's *really* uncomfortable!

Now a word about the saddle itself. New bikes come with the saddle set so that it's perfectly level. You may find a level saddle comfortable. If not, you can change its angle by loosening the bolt that attaches the saddle to its support post. You can see the bolt in the illustration. It's right above the cyclist's left hand.

Once the bolt is loosened, you may tilt the saddle forward or backward. Some riders like a backward tilt, but this isn't advised because it tends to move your body weight away from the center of the bike. Pedaling and control then become a fraction more difficult. No matter which tilt you choose, be sure to make the angle a very slight one, no more than a fraction of an inch. Too much angle gives you the feeling that you're slipping off the saddle. You then automatically tighten your muscles to lock yourself in place. The result? A sore rear end.

In general, your handlebars will be at a comfortable height if they're approximately level with the saddle. This will enable you to lean slightly forward, at anything from a 10- to a 45-degree angle. It's far less tiring to lean forward than to ride sitting straight up. This position also places your weight over the center of the frame and makes the bike easier to control.

The handlebars can be adjusted as easily as the seat. As the illustration shows, they're connected to the frame by a metal stem that rises out of the head tube and turns into a gooseneck. The bars themselves are clamped to the gooseneck and held securely in place by a bolt.

To raise or lower the bars, you must adjust the hexagonal bolt located at the point where the stem becomes the gooseneck. Loosen the bolt about two

ADJUSTING HANDLEBAR HEIGHT

turns. Then tap the head of the bolt with your wrench to loosen an interior lock nut that helps to hold the stem in place. Now try moving the stem to different heights until you find the one that's most comfortable for you. Be sure that the gooseneck is facing straight forward over the front wheel when you tighten the hexagonal bolt for the last time.

Again, a caution: just as you did with the seat, make certain that the handlebar stem extends at least two inches inside the frame after you've made your final adjustment. With less than two inches, the stem could come out as you're sailing along. And—great fun—you'd be without a "steering wheel."

Should you wish to raise or lower the angle of the handlebars, you can do so by loosening the bolt that holds them to the gooseneck.

You can try a simple test for proper handlebar height if you have a ten-speed bike or a bike with similar handlebars. As you did when looking for the right seat height, sit on your bike while a friend holds it upright for you. Take a comfortable position, leaning forward and placing your hands on the topmost part of the bars. Now pull one hand away and swing your arm backward. Let your shoulder and torso ride back with it. Then bring your arm forward. Let it swing naturally and in a relaxed fashion. If your hand returns right to the handlebar, you're all set. If it comes up below and in front of the bars, they're set too low. If it rises behind them, they're too high. Make whatever adjustment is needed.

Now, to finish things off, let's mention that word *comfortable* again. It's the most important word of all, and it's a very personal one. Only you—and you alone—will know when you're comfortable. So please remember that all these suggestions for proper bike fit are general ones. Treat them only as guides to help you adjust your bike to a fit that makes you happy. Touring is fun, yes. But it's most fun only when you're comfortable.

ALL RIGHT. YOUR bike fits nicely. You're comfortable there in the saddle. It's time for your first tour.

CHAPTER 2

Your First Tours: Making Plans

THERE'S AN OLD
saying that a baby must learn to crawl before trying
to walk. Similarly, a new swimmer must get the hang
of floating before attempting to stroke. The same goes
for you as a cyclist. As we said right at the start, your
first tours should be short ones. Use them for fun and
for building the strength and experience you'll need for
future adventures. Let them last no more than a few
hours.

TOUR PLANS

No matter how short your first tours may be, they
should be planned ahead of time. You can run into all
sorts of headaches out there on the road if you don't

plan ahead, and your trip can end in disappointment. For instance, you might take a wrong turn and end up lost. Or you might be without a snack at the very time when you want it most. Or you could stop for a rest in a dusty spot when, just a mile up the road, there's a great picnic area that you didn't know about.

Now the idea of sitting down and planning a tour may turn you off at first. It may sound a little too much like doing homework. But it's really not. Give it a try and you'll find out. The planning is all part of the fun. In fact, practically all cyclists will tell you that it's more than half the fun.

Furthermore, there's nothing difficult about planning a short tour. All you need do is take four common-sense steps, the same ones you'll take when the time comes to plan a long trip. Begin by deciding where to go.

STEP ONE: PICK A DESTINATION

You may want to cycle to a certain spot with friends, perhaps to a picnic grounds or a picturesque village. Or you may simply want to head into the countryside, travel as far as you can, and turn back when everyone agrees that it's time to go home. Either way is fine. It's up to you, and it all depends on what will give you and your companions the most cycling pleasure.

It's probably best, though, to have a destination in mind. This gives you a goal and helps you to keep pedaling. And you will feel a sense of accomplishment when you reach your destination. If you don't get there on your first try, you still face the challenge of trying to do better next time.

Just be sure to pick a destination that you think you can reach and return from in the time allotted for your trip. The thing to avoid is a destination so far away that you'll be caught in the dark coming home. Night riding is dangerous unless you're an experienced cyclist and unless you're adequately equipped. Always plan to leave after the sun comes up and return before it goes down.

Exactly how far should you plan to travel and still be certain of arriving home before nightfall? The answer is up to you and your friends. It all depends on your strength at present and on the many touring factors that can speed you up or slow you down—factors such as the condition of the roads and the number of hills to be climbed.

You can get some idea of a good distance by looking at the day-long trips that bicycle clubs offer for beginners. The trips usually run somewhere in the range of ten to thirty miles (experienced cyclists think nothing of traveling between a hundred and two hundred miles a day). Why not take a look at your present strength and pick what seems to be a reasonable distance within this beginning range? As best you can, settle on a distance that you think you can cover without becoming overly tired.

Mind you, I said *overly* tired. Getting tired is a part of cycling. You just can't pedal all day without knowing that you've worked your muscles and used up plenty of energy. But it's a good tiredness. What you want to avoid is the exhaustion that so many beginners suffer. It can take all the pleasure out of your first trip, leave you with a variety of unnecessary aches and pains, and turn you off for future tours.

Don't be embarrassed about starting modestly. Remember, your first jaunts are meant to give you a day's worth of fun and build your strength and skill for future trips. Look on them as test runs. Build your strength slowly and steadily. One of these days, you'll be fit for distances that may now seem impossible. And one of these days, like many cyclists, you may find it a challenge to test yourself and push yourself right to the limit of your endurance—but not now.

In fact, it's best to be "underambitious" on your first trip and risk picking a distance that's too short. So what if you arrive home a bit too early? That's better than struggling the last miles in exhaustion, and in darkness. Experience will soon show you how far you can travel in a day.

A friend of mine who has toured for years has a first-trip suggestion that you might want to follow. He advises you to pick your distance and then cut it in half. The chances are, he says, that you'll then be right on target for a tour you can easily handle.

Here are three more special tips for helping you plan the distance. They'll also be of help on all your future tours.

First, if you're planning a trip in the fall or winter, remember that the days are shorter than in the summer. You'll have to reduce your mileage if you hope to be home by dark.

Second, learn about the prevailing wind directions in your area. Suppose that you know the wind will be in your face in the morning when you're fresh, and at your back when you're riding home. You may be able to plan a longer trip because you can count on the wind giving you a welcome push at the time you're growing tired. You may want to plan a shorter trip if you find that you're going to be fighting a strong breeze on the homeward leg.

Later, when you're making tours that last for several days, you will want to know the prevailing wind directions in the areas through which you pass. You'll then know when to expect the wind to work against you and when to expect its help.

Finally, think about the spot where your tour is to begin. Let's say that you have in mind a jaunt along a certain country road. If you live close by and can start your tour from your home, great. But what if you have to pedal across town to your starting point—or carry your bike there by car, bus, or streetcar? And then return home the same way? You will need extra time. Be sure to figure this into the number of hours you plan for the trip.

STEP TWO: PICK YOUR ROUTE

There may be just one route that will lead you to and from your destination. Fine. You'll have to use it. But, more than likely, there will be several ways to get where you're going. You'll want to pick the one that strikes you as best.

Your search for that route begins with a map. For day-long tours, you should turn to a local map— perhaps of your county or your town and its surrounding areas. A local map is better than a state or regional one because it has the space to include all the available roads, streets, and even lanes. You can buy local maps at most gasoline stations. They can often be purchased at your city hall or county offices. Sometimes, they're to be had without charge from the city or county.

If you're very lucky and have bike trails in your area, be sure to check with your local parks and recreation department. You're almost certain to find a map there that shows all the trails. If no map is available, you can talk to the employees on duty. They'll be able to give you plenty of information about the trails. One way or the other, you'll probably come away with ideas for many a tour.

But let's get back to the local map. As you study it to seek a good bike route, you should keep a few general rules in mind. To begin, try not to choose roads that are marked by heavy black or red lines and that seem to run a pretty straight course from one place to another. These are main roads—wide arterials, highways, and freeways. They carry heavy, high-speed auto and truck traffic—the cyclist's greatest enemy. Also, in many states, freeways and main highways are closed to bikes.

At the opposite end of the scale, do what you can to avoid selecting roads that appear as squiggly lines. This means that they're narrow back roads. You can count on them winding their way through one little curve after another because they were once trails that followed the shape of the land. They follow the paths of streams, gorges, hillsides, and even old cow trails. And the chances are that they're in poor condition. If you choose them, you may be in for an overly long, back-breaking ride that may even do some damage to your bike.

In general, your best choices are secondary roads. On the map, they appear as clearly drawn, narrow lines that fall about midway between the heavily marked highways and the squiggly back-breakers. They're good for cycling because they don't carry as much heavy traffic as the bigger roadways.

But there is a cycling rule that you should observe right from the start. Always try to find the widest of the secondary roads for your trips. Though perhaps they do not carry heavy traffic, the secondaries have their share of speeders. All roads do. The wider the road is, the farther you'll be from the passing cars and trucks as you pedal on or near the shoulder—and the safer you'll be.

Of course, it's impossible to tell from a map whether one secondary is wider than another. You're going to have to ask for information from someone who has traveled over the roads before. And you're going to have to keep your eyes open whenever you're riding in the family car. When you see a road that looks good, remember it—especially if it has a broad, paved shoulder. It will be a great one for future use.

When you begin to check the secondary roads on the map, you should be alert to a number of points. Do you, for instance, see any markings for hills? Do they lie across your path? You may not wish to do much climbing on your first rides. If so, search for roads that will avoid most of the hills—or at least the steepest ones. And always remember that hills have to be figured into your time estimate because they slow you down.

Likewise, look for various points of interest. Most local maps show the locations of picnic grounds, historical landmarks, county parks, vista points, streams, and so forth. Places of interest such as these do much to add to the fun of a tour. Though two routes may seem alike on the map, one of them may be just right because it runs past a picnic area that would be great for a snack or lunch break. Or one might have a historical landmark that would be interesting to see, or a vista point that would be perfect for a rest stop. As you sit there and relax, you can enjoy the sweeping view of a valley or a forest.

Also, be sure to see if any towns lie in your path. You may want to cycle into a town for lunch at a restaurant or for a visit to some interesting spot. If so, fine. But town riding can be a pain for a cyclist because of all the car traffic. So, if there's a town along the way, you might want to look for a route that carries you clear of the downtown area or swings you around the outskirts so that you miss the town altogether.

There's hardly a doubt that a few minutes with the map will show you several routes to your destination. Perhaps they'll all look equally inviting. That means just one thing: you now have a series of short tours that you can take over the next weeks or months.

Before you can settle on the one that you want to try first, you'll need to know the distance covered by each route. Now is the time to turn to the map's *legend,* which is usually located at the bottom of the map or in one corner. As you know, every map is drawn to scale—perhaps a scale of one inch to every five miles or a quarter-inch for every mile—and the legend shows the scale that's used on your map.

Working with a ruler, measure the distance along each route to your destination. Perhaps one or two routes look as if they can be easily reached in the time allotted for your journey. Perhaps another two or three seem a bit too long for comfort. Take your pick from the best of the shorter routes. Save the longer ones for later.

But suppose that they all seem too long. Then simply pick a new destination along the route—one that's closer to home. Remember, it's always smart to be "underambitious" on your first tour.

Step Three: Check Your Route

There's a very old rule in cycling. It's followed by everyone, from the newest bikers to the most experienced tourers and racers. Before ever hitting the road, learn all that you can about your route. Never—but *never*— pedal out on a route that you're totally unfamiliar with. Every road has its share of problems. It's safest to know about them ahead of time.

The best way to learn a route—or to make your final selection if you haven't yet come to a decision— is to travel over it. Ask your parents if they'll drive you along the route in the family car. This shouldn't be too much trouble to arrange, especially if you ask well in advance, because just a few miles are involved. As you sit in the car, be alert to every passing thing. Watch the road for chuckholes, curves, bumps, patches of gravel, and so forth; these obstacles can give you trouble if you encounter them suddenly. Watch to see if there's a paved shoulder that will make riding easier and at the same time keep you well away from passing car traffic. Count the hills. Check for spots that will make good, comfortable rest stops. Keep an eye out for restaurants where you might stop for lunch or a snack. Do you spot any public telephones? Remember where they are. You might need them to call home if your bike breaks down and can't be fixed at the roadside.

If you're unable to drive over the route ahead of

time, then turn to the many people who may be able to tell you something about it—yourself included. If you've driven over it at some earlier date, call it to mind as best you can. How about your parents? How about classmates who have relatives living out in that direction? Your city parks and recreation department may be of help.

And don't forget the police department, the state troopers, or the highway patrol. They always have all sorts of road information. Also, remember that they must be called if you're thinking about going part of the way on a main highway. They'll quickly tell you whether your bike is permitted on it. If any main road is off limits to you, they'll be able to suggest an alternate route.

One of your best bets is the local bike club, if your town has one. You can be sure that the members have tried every road in the area. They'll be happy not only to tell you about them but also to give you some helpful tips on how best to handle them. On top of all else, you may end up joining the club and sharing in its tours. If you don't have a bike club at hand, you might try a bicycle shop. Most bicycle shop owners are themselves enthusiastic riders and should have much information of value.

And another good idea: when choosing your companions for the ride, why not try to find someone who has already biked over the route. He or she can then serve as your guide.

And so, in a word, turn to anyone who can help

you with the route. Do all that you can to familiarize yourself with what lies ahead. You'll then be set up for a safe and pleasant ride. Remember one of cycling's basic rules: never head out on a route that's totally unfamiliar to you.

STEP FOUR: MAKE A MAP

Even on the shortest of tours, you should carry a map. This isn't because you're apt to get lost, though that's always a possibility. Rather, a map is the one sure item that will keep you from making a wrong turn and going a couple of miles out of your way before you discover your mistake. Quite as important, a map is a fine aid in helping you to judge how far you've traveled and how much farther you have to go.

Once you've settled on your route, you can prepare your map in either of two ways: you can trace the route in ink or heavy pencil on the map you've been using, or you can draw a map of your own.

I prefer to make a map of my own, and so do most of my cyclist friends. For one thing, it's fun to draw. For another, it affords you plenty of space for marking in road names, distances, and so forth.

There's nothing to making a map of a short trip. Using your regular map as a guide, draw your route on a sheet of paper. Draw it as much to a scale of your choosing as you can. Mark the names or the

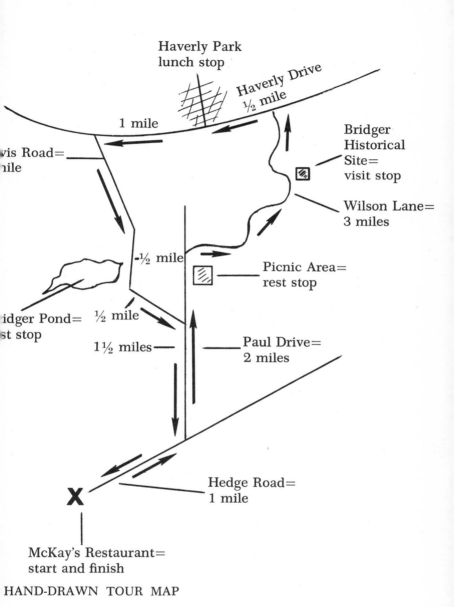

Haverly Park
lunch stop

Haverly Drive
½ mile

1 mile

Bridger
Historical
Site=
visit stop

...vis Road=
...ile

Wilson Lane=
3 miles

-½ mile

Picnic Area=
rest stop

...idger Pond=
...st stop

½ mile

1½ miles

Paul Drive=
2 miles

Hedge Road=
1 mile

X

McKay's Restaurant=
start and finish

HAND-DRAWN TOUR MAP

county numbers of the roadways alongside them. Put in the names of the spots along the way that will serve as landmarks, rest stops, and places you'd like to see. Finally, include the distances between points along the way, as shown in the illustration. These distances are especially helpful, showing you exactly where you are at any time in the journey.

Of course, don't forget to carry the map with you once you've gone to the trouble of drawing it. It can be easily carried somewhere in your clothing. A breast or hip pocket is a good choice because it's easily reached. And, above all, don't throw the map away when you get home. You may want to use it again in the future.

Also, if you're like most cyclists, you'll want to keep a record of all your trips. Your maps will be a basic part of that record. In addition, your record can include a list of the mileages and cycling times for your jaunts so that you can see that you've traveled greater distances and posted better times as the weeks and months rolled by. You can also include notes on the sights you've seen, the flowers that have blossomed at different times of the year, the way the trees have changed with the seasons, and the birds and animals that have watched you glide past. And, of course, you may want to put in the photographs that you've taken along the way.

For many cyclists, a record of their tours is an absolute must. It's the history of their cycling adventures. They've spent endless happy hours building their records and then poring over them to relive all those good hours on the road. You can do the same.

ONCE YOU'VE PICKED your destination, checked your route, and drawn your map, you have put the basic planning for your tour out of the way. Only some final preparations remain. They'll make you ready for the road.

CHAPTER 3

Your First Tours: Ready for the Road

YOUR FINAL PREPARATIONS will see you doing a variety of jobs. They're the very chores that you'll also have to take care of for a longer tour. They range from choosing your riding companions to collecting your travel gear and packing it aboard your bike.

Let's talk first about your companions.

CHOOSING YOUR COMPANIONS

There's nothing to stop you from touring alone if that's what you'd like to do. But it's always good to have friends with you as you pedal along. You can enjoy their company. You can share with them the beauty of the passing scenery. And don't forget that they're great to have around should your bike break down or should you hurt yourself in a spill.

You can pick your companions after you've made your tour plans or at any time during the planning stages. Or you may want to choose them right away and then make your plans together. It's all up to you. You may be the kind of person who likes to work things out alone. Or you may be the type who enjoys getting some help.

It's best to make your first trips with just one friend, or perhaps two (and don't forget that your parents may be great choices). You should avoid getting too enthusiastic and asking the whole neighborhood or your entire class to come along. A large group can be clumsy to handle at times. You'll need to gather some cycling experience before trying to lead many people.

To ensure that your first rides will be as enjoyable as possible, you should choose your friends with care. Actually, you should keep two points firmly in mind when you make your choice.

First, pick someone who is about equal to you in physical strength and riding skill. If two travelers are not well matched in these ways, the weaker one will constantly fall behind and have to struggle to keep up. The stronger one will be forced to pedal slowly so as not to cycle out of sight. There's nothing like slow pedaling to tire the strongest of riders. So you're both going to be worn out and discouraged in short order. Interest in the trip will evaporate, and the day's fun will be spoiled.

Second, take a close look at your companion's personality before asking him or her to come along. Look to see if this friend has what is called "the cyclist's personality." Is he or she the cheerful type? Is this the kind of person who will remain interested in the trip that's been planned? Will this friend be willing to keep plugging away on those pedals when the going gets a bit tough? If the answer is yes on all counts, you've found the perfect companion.

But if your friend promises to be any of the following types, then you should think twice about your invitation. Is your friend a Sammy Saddlesore who will begin to complain as soon as the aches and pains show themselves? Or a Betty Boredom who will quickly lose interest in the trip and decide that it would be great fun to hang around a restaurant for the rest of the day? Or, worst of all, a Gertie Give-up who will collapse at the first sign of tiredness and demand to go home?

Any of these characters can ruin the day for you. Fortunately, they can be sighted long before you get on the road. Their everyday behavior is the tip-off. If some of your friends are always moaning about school and life in general, you can bet that they'll be moaners on a tour. So keep your eyes open and pick with care. Always look for a friend who is as strong and skilled on a bike as you. Always look for that

GUS AND GERTIE GIVE-UP
cheerful someone who will have a good time wherever the tour goes and who will cooperate in making the day a success.

COLLECTING YOUR GEAR

Your gear includes everything from clothing to the tools needed to repair your bike, should it break down. No matter how long you plan to be on the road, you must always keep the weight of your gear at a minimum. Too much weight can make a bike hard to handle.

For a tour of just a few hours, of course, only a small amount of gear is needed. As far as clothing is concerned, dress yourself comfortably, either in everyday wear or in cycling shorts and jersey. Be sure to wear comfortable shoes. It's a good idea to carry along a lightweight windbreaker or sweater in case the air cools or a wind comes up.

Incidentally, if you choose not to carry anything extra, there's a simple way to keep warm if the temperature drops. Just put a sheet or two of folded newspaper under your shirt and against your chest. Since the chest is so exposed to the wind, it's the part of the body that usually suffers most from the cold. The newspaper will do a nice job of protecting it.

If you wear shorts and jersey, you're likely to pick up a sunburn on your legs, arms, and the back of your neck. Coat yourself lightly with a protective lotion before you leave. Then carry the lotion with you so that you can make fresh applications during the trip. As you ride, you will perspire, the lotion will wash away, and you'll need some more.

Whether you're in shorts and jersey or everyday clothing, there is one piece of cycling equipment that you definitely should have: a protective helmet. Made of plastic or leather, it can be purchased inexpensively at any bike shop. If you don't yet own a helmet, be sure to get one as soon as possible. It can save you from a bad injury as a result of a traffic accident or a spill.

Among the things you'll need to carry is equipment for repairs, should your bike break down. Fortunately, the repair gear can be kept at a bare minimum for the present. Usually, the worst problem that you'll encounter on a short tour is a flat tire.

You'll need an air pump, a patch kit, and the few tools necessary to remove the wheel and then the tire. As its name indicates, the kit contains rubber patches used to mend the tire's inner tube. The kit and the pump can be purchased for just a few dollars. When buying the pump, make certain that it fits your tire valve before you hand any money to the sales clerk. For a little extra, you can buy a pump that attaches to the bike frame.

As for tools, you'll be wise to purchase a tool kit, though a few moments in your garage may turn up all the tools you need. Basically, you must have a wrench to get the wheel off the bike and a couple of small tire irons to remove the tire from the rim. The

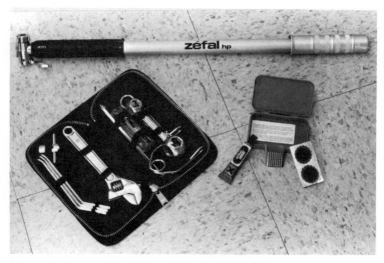

AIR PUMP, TOOL KIT, AND PATCH KIT.

irons are bent strips of metal, usually not more than six inches long.

Whether you use a tool kit or tools that you find at home, you should take the time to practice changing a tire before you head for the road. You'll then know exactly what to do if you run into trouble. You'll save yourself many a minute of frustration out there on the roadside.

The practice will also show you whether you've got the right tools from home or in your kit for the job. Always remember that not every kit fits every bike. At the time you buy a kit, be sure to tell the sales clerk the make of your bike. The clerk will then be able to give you a kit with a proper fit. But check it with a practice session anyway, just to make certain. If the kit is not right, return it to the clerk and insist on one that will work properly.

In Chapter 10, we'll talk more of how you go about the actual job of repairing a tire.

If you own a ten-speed bike, you should carry along an extra rear brake cable and an extra rear derailleur cable (in case the word *derailleur* is unfamiliar to you, there will be more about it in the next chapter). Though the ten-speed has brake and derailleur cables on both the front and rear wheels, you need take only the rear ones, which are long enough to work also on the front wheel. (The front cables don't have enough length to stretch to the rear wheel.) In addition, carry the tool kit that's advised for the bike.

How About Food?

Food is no problem on a short jaunt. You can take along a lunch if you wish. Or you can buy lunch at a restaurant or pick up what you need at a grocery store somewhere.

Just be sure to follow one suggestion: always eat lightly when on tour. Heavy foods make you feel too sluggish for effective pedaling. So, should you drop by a restaurant, turn up your nose at those giant hamburgers, sizzling french fries, and thick milk shakes. Choose something like a bowl of soup, a salad, or a vegetarian sandwich instead. If you pack a lunch, you'll find that a simple sandwich, some fruit, and water or fruit juice will do just fine.

It's a good idea, too, to start the day with a light and nutritious breakfast. Save your heavy eating until you return home. With all the energy that's gone into working those pedals, you'll really enjoy your evening meal.

You'll need some snacks to nibble on from time to time as you pedal. Snacks not only provide enjoyment but also help to keep your energy high. Your best choices here are fruit bars, dehydrated fruit slices, granola tidbits, raisins, and nuts. Just take your pick and store them in your pockets so that you can reach them at any time. Please don't—repeat, *please don't*—use candy as a snack, even if some cyclists swear by it. The heavy sugar content in candy lifts your energy—yes. But it then can let you down with a real thump, leaving you more tired than before.

Be sure to carry water. Despite all the juices on the market today, water is still the world's finest thirst quencher. And it certainly beats orange juice when the time comes to wash your hands after lunch or after a tire repair. Water is best stored in a plastic bottle that can be clamped to the bike frame. The attachment bottle costs next to nothing at any bike shop. If you don't wish to invest in the bottle, then perhaps there's a canteen around the house that you can use. For obvious reasons, never carry water in a glass bottle or jar.

PLASTIC WATER BOTTLE ON BIKE FRAME

PACKING YOUR BIKE

Once you've collected all your gear, it's time to pack it aboard your bike. Once again, because you're going to be away for such a short time, you're up against no problem at all. But you should take as much care with the packing as you would before leaving for a week-long ride. Packing is fun, and it's great practice for the future.

To make sure that nothing is forgotten, why not start with a list of your gear? You can check each item as you collect it for packing. Your list will probably look something like this:

Map
Lunch
Energy snacks
Water
Tire pump
Patch kit
Tools for tire repair
Riding helmet
Windbreaker or sweater
Protective sun lotion

If you own a ten-speed, don't forget to include the rear brake and derailleur cables and the tool kit necessary for repairs. And, no matter what kind of bike you ride, three more items should be on the list: money, a compass, and a first-aid kit.

Money is a must even on the shortest trips and

even if you're carrying a lunch. You may want to buy a snack along the way. More important, you should always have money to see you through an emergency. But how much? I would suggest at least five dollars. Ten would be better.

As for the compass, it can be a real help if you become lost or miss a turn and begin to suspect that you're riding in the wrong direction. Along with your map, it's the best piece of equipment around for getting you back on track. On top of all else, it can be fun to check the direction of your travel from time to time.

And it's obvious that a first-aid kit will be a great help when you have to tend to some scrape or bruise after a spill. Incidentally, as your tours become longer and longer, it will be a good idea to take a first-aid course. You never can tell when it will come in handy.

Now for packing your bike: you can carry your map and snacks, of course, in your pockets; attach the plastic water bottle and tire pump to the bike frame, if possible; then place everything else in a small bag.

In a later chapter, we're going to be talking about the types of carriers that can be used for storage on long trips. They range from what are called pannier bags to handlebar bags and saddlebags. If you already have one of these containers, there's nothing to stop you from using it on a short trip. Because of your small amount of gear, the handlebar bag will probably be the most helpful of all. But let's say that you're without any sort of carrier. What can you do?

Look around the house to see if you can find any type of small cloth or canvas bag. A small duffle bag —sometimes called a ditty bag—of the sort that campers use for their cosmetics or shaving equipment would be a nice find. So would a canvas airline bag. If your search leaves you empty-handed, then a piece of sturdy cloth or canvas will serve well. Just wrap your things securely in it. Don't worry if it's not a large piece. You'll be surprised how much gear can be compressed into a small package. In fact, you should always try to compress everything into the smallest package possible.

Once the gear is packaged, you can place it on the luggage rack over your rear wheel or tie it to the underside of your saddle.

Whether you use the rack or the underside of the saddle, make sure that the package is fastened securely. You don't want it shifting or dropping to one side of the wheel and perhaps tangling itself in the spokes as you pedal. And you can guess how discouraging it is to glance over your shoulder and see all your things lying on the road about a quarter of a mile back.

It's best not to tie the package down with string or rope. String breaks too easily. Unless you're an expert at fashioning knots in a rope, you'll find that they have the bad habit of loosening as time goes by.

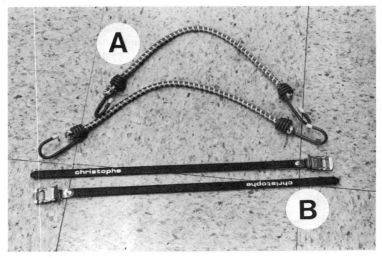

BUNGEE STRAP AND TOE CLIP STRAPS

Also, it's a pain to fiddle with the knots every time you want to get to your gear.

You'll be happiest if you use leather straps of some sort, preferably with buckles or clips. The bungee strap (Figure A in the illustration) is a good choice. Your bike may be equipped with toe clips, which always come with two extra straps (Figure B). You'll want to have the extras along as replacements. They can do double duty by holding your things in place.

CHECKING YOUR BIKE

One last job remains. You should check your bike to see that it's ready for the road. The check may seem unnecessary because you're planning such a short trip.

But it's vital to a safe outing. All good cyclists make the check before every ride. Right from the start, you should get into the habit of imitating them.

The check usually takes just a few minutes. The following tips will help see you through the job:

1. Check to see that the wheels, pedals, and all adjustable parts of the frame (the seat post, for instance) are bolted securely in place. While checking the wheels, see that the front one is pointing straight ahead.

2. Be sure that the wheels spin easily. If they seem at all tight, add some lubricant to the hubs.

3. Make certain that the wheel spokes are secure at the points where they join the rim. Tighten any that appear to be loose.

4. See that the tires are in good condition and that they're inflated to the correct pressure. The amount of pressure needed can usually be found printed on the tire wall. If you're without a pressure gauge, you can test the tires by pushing each wheel against a curb. Each tire should "squish" out a bit, but not so much that you can feel the rim go against the curb. If you're blessed with strong hands, try pinching the tire between thumb and forefinger. The tire should give a little. Your thumb and forefinger, however, shouldn't be able to touch each other.

5. Check to see that your gears are operating properly if you have a three- or a ten-speed bike. Should there seem to be a problem, check your owner's manual for advice on correcting it.

6. Examine your brakes. Ride up and down the driveway or a quiet street for a few moments to see that they're responding the way you want them to. The brakes are the single most important piece of equipment on your bike. Don't leave home unless you know they're in good shape. It's the only safe thing to do.

AND THAT'S IT. All the planning and all the preparations for your tour are now at an end. So away you go —out to the open road.

CHAPTER 4

On the Road

THERE ARE RIGHT ways and wrong ways to handle a bicycle. Naturally, you'll want to use the right ones when you take to the road. They're called *riding techniques,* and they make it possible for you to get the most out of your bike. They also bring you home safely and much less tired than you would otherwise be.

Starting with the proper way to pedal, we're going to look at these various techniques in the next pages. Incidentally, don't wait until you're on tour to try them. They'll serve you just as well on everyday runs to school and the store.

PEDALING "ALL THE WAY AROUND."

PEDALING

Good pedaling depends on two techniques. First, you must have a smooth stroking action. Second, you need to stroke along at a steady pace.

Most beginners do not have a smooth stroking action. They do fine at the start of the stroke, pushing down on the pedal as it moves forward and swings into its descent. But they stop pushing as soon as they reach bottom. Then, once the pedal is rising again, they let their foot rest on it while the other foot is pushing down on the opposite pedal. This is very tiring—and quickly so—because each leg is made to work unnecessarily hard. In its turn, each not only pushes down on its pedal but also lifts the weight of the resting foot.

You'll do much to conserve your energy if you develop the habit of pedaling "all the way around" on each stroke. Here's how it works. When the pedal is just beyond the top of its circle (Picture A), push it forward and down. On reaching bottom, don't stop pushing. Apply some more pressure for another instant (Picture B), moving the pedal backward until it starts to rise. Now further pushing becomes impossible, but don't let your foot sit there and rest. Lift it a bit. You needn't come clear off the pedal. Just pull the foot up enough to remove the weight.

You may find it a little difficult to pedal "all the way around" at first. Your foot will always want to rest, and you'll need to exert some effort to lift it even slightly. You'll feel some tiredness, but don't give up. A little practice will take care of things. Once the beginning tiredness has disappeared, you'll find yourself able to pedal comfortably for longer distances than ever before.

Now let's talk for a moment about a special piece of cycling equipment—toe clips. Consisting of metal springs and cloth straps, these devices can be attached to the pedals. They fit over your toes and hold your feet in position against the pedals. You'll find clips especially helpful because they allow you to do more than lift your foot on the upstroke. With your feet anchored in place, you can actually pull each pedal upward and thus reduce still further the amount of pushing done by the opposite foot.

As a tourer, you'll be wise to invest in toe clips. There's a question as to when you should buy them, however. Some cyclists advise that you wait until you're an expert rider; they believe that the clips are dangerous because, with your feet anchored down, you may not be able to free yourself fast enough to use your leg as a brace, should you go off balance. Other cyclists argue that the clips don't hold your feet so securely that you can't break away in plenty of time. So the decision as to when to buy clips must be left to you. You probably won't need them for your first short trips, but you'll find them a great help when you begin to pedal long distances.

One last point about your stroking action.

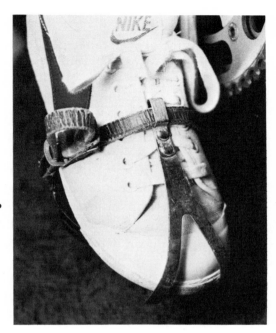

A TOE CLIP

Along with remembering to pedal "all the way around," be sure always to work with the balls of your feet on the pedals. Avoid pedaling with your arches or heels. The balls of your feet enable you to exert the best pressure possible, with the result that fatigue doesn't come on so quickly. And you have the chance to develop the technique known as "ankling." When ankling, you flex your foot downward as the pedal descends. Then you flex the foot upward on the upstroke. This technique provides you with extra pedaling power.

Now let's talk about pedaling at a steady pace. Everyone likes to vary the rate of speed, sometimes going fast, sometimes slowing down. This is fine. But, when riding for any distance, you should try to pedal at a steady rate whenever you can—*and with as little effort as possible*. In general, you'll find yourself less tired if you pedal steadily rather than pump hard one minute and then laze along the next.

It's difficult to pedal steadily with little effort on a one-speed bike. When you encounter even a slight hill, there's no lower gear to help make the climb easier. You simply have to bear down harder with the old feet. Much the same is true of the three-speed with its few gears. And so only one thing can be said: for easy pedaling on a one- or three-speed, you must make sure that your bike fits you and that you keep it in the best shape possible, seeing in particular that it's always well lubricated so that the wheels turn effortlessly. Lubrication, of course, is also necessary for the ten-speed, which can be tough to handle if the wheels are tight. But the one-speed and the three-speed are truly difficult here.

When riding a ten-speed, you should pedal not only steadily but also at a rather fast rate. Cycling studies have shown that you'll do best if you pedal somewhere in the range of 60 to 100 revolutions per minute (rpm). A pace of under 60 rpm can strain the muscles, tire them quickly, and bring on soreness. And, unless you're a very well-trained rider, you'll have trouble maintaining a rate of over 100 rpm for long without tiring.

The gears on a ten-speed bike enable you to stay in the 60 to 100 rpm range regardless of the terrain.

You can hit 60 to 100 when you're in a high gear on flat ground and traveling at about 20 to 25 miles an hour. By shifting to a lower gear, you can continue in the same range while climbing a hill at perhaps 3 to 5 miles an hour. And here you can see the best example of why the ten-speed is so great for touring. It lets you pedal to top efficiency practically all the time.

But where in the 60 to 100 range should you pedal? Only you can find the answer. Practice will show you the actual rate that, depending on your strength, is most comfortable. Also, you may have some trouble hitting 60 rpm on your first rides. Practice will build your strength so that you'll eventually reach—and then go well beyond—the 60 rpm mark.

As you practice, you must concentrate on avoiding one beginner's mistake. On going into high gear, you'll be tempted to take life easy and pedal slowly. You may think you're conserving energy with those slow strokes. The reverse is true. Remember, pedaling at a rate of less than 60 rpm is tiring.

Why? When you pedal slowly in high gear (or in any gear, for that matter), you take a longer time to send each pedal around in a full circle. You then do far more work for each stroke and exert far more energy. So continue to pedal quickly and steadily. Each stroke will take less work. You'll last longer before growing tired.

If you don't want to take my word for this, then watch some experienced cyclists as they pedal in high gear. They'll look rather strange. Their legs will be going around quite quickly and you'll think that the bikes should be whizzing along. But they'll be moving at a comparatively slow, but steady, rate.

Like a stroke that carries you "all the way around," steady and well-paced pedaling is hard to learn, and for much the same reason. It will at first seem difficult to drive your feet around quickly and continuously in those tight little circles. But, if you'll practice a few minutes each day and try to pedal steadily whenever you cycle to school or the store, you'll soon get the hang of things.

HANDLING THE BRAKES

A variety of brakes are made for bicycles. Most often, though, you'll find just two types: the coaster and the caliper. Your trusty one-speed will be equipped with coaster brakes. Caliper brakes are found on gear bikes.

Coaster brakes are the easiest things in the world to operate. All you do to work them is reverse the direction of the pedals. This causes the rear wheel to slow its turning. It grips the pavement and brings you to a stop.

Caliper brakes are operated by pressing two levers set across from each other on the handlebars. The levers are connected to brake shoes—little pads that hang on either side of the wheel rims from a crescent-shaped clamp—by means of long cables. One cable, as seen in the illustration, leads to the

CALIPER BRAKES

front wheel; the other goes to the rear wheel. When you work the levers, the cables drive the pads against the rims and force the wheels to stop turning.

Some ten-speed bikes come equipped with disc brakes. They, too, are operated by levers on the handlebars. Discs work efficiently, but many cyclists advise against them for touring. They're on the heavy side and add extra weight that can be tiring on a long haul.

No matter what kind of brakes you use, if you want to develop good cycling technique, you should keep one point constantly in mind: *always apply the brakes as gently and as steadily as you can.* Never slam them on unless an emergency forces you to do so. "Slamming" stops are great ways to end up in a skid and a flight over the handlebars. Remember: no grandstanding for watching friends and no pretending that you're a stunt person—unless you're among the funny ones who enjoy gathering a collection of scrapes and bruises.

Even when faced with an emergency, try to use as gentle a touch as possible. If there's time for it, do all you can to apply the braking pressure smoothly and steadily. Try to stop in time without standing the bike on end. If there's not time, then you must take your chances with a hard, slamming stop. You may take a bad fall, but that's better than crashing into the side of a truck.

One tip for emergency stops: as you hit the brakes, pull back with your body, rising a little off the saddle as you do so and straightening your arms. Pulling back helps to slow the bike a little and offers some protection against a trip across the handlebars. It also pulls your face back and may save you from sailing nose-first into the side of that truck.

The best tip of all: always be alert and ride carefully so that emergency stops are rarely—or, better yet, never—a part of your cycling experience.

When riding a three- or a ten-speed bike, remember to press both brake levers gently at the same time. Then, depending on the type of stop you're making, you may want to add an extra degree of pressure to the front or rear wheel. Extra pressure on the rear wheel brings you to a slower stop—a "dragging" one—because the wheel has little weight over it and thus doesn't offer much traction. The front wheel, with the rider leaning forward, bears a great deal of weight and has very strong traction. Extra pressure on the front brake causes the bike to stop more quickly.

When applying pressure to the rear wheel, try not to go so far that you lock the wheel. A locked wheel can send the bike into a skid. Also, avoid pressing hard on one brake while leaving the other one alone. Hard pressure on the front brake alone can send the bike up on end or turn the wheel to the side; in either case, you're set for an unscheduled tour across the handlebars. Like a locked wheel, hard pressure on the rear brake threatens a skid.

If you own a brand-new three- or ten-speed, be sure to check the brakes before your first ride. Make certain that they're working properly and, in particular, learn which lever controls which wheel. You can be in for trouble if you need to add a great deal of pressure to the rear wheel only to find that you're working the front-wheel lever instead. Another unscheduled tour may be in the works. On most bikes, the front-wheel lever is located on the right handlebar. But take no chances. Check to be sure.

Also, you'll be wise to practice with the brakes before taking your new bike out for a run. Using an open space, ride at different speeds and try the brakes, sometimes merely slowing the bike and sometimes bringing it to a stop. Learn exactly how the brakes respond to various amounts of hand pressure. Teach yourself to apply a gentle, even pressure rather than a hard, jerky one. Once you know what you can do with the brakes, you will be ready for the road. Then, wherever you ride, concentrate on developing your braking skills so that you're always able to stop smoothly and safely.

Whether you're riding with coasters or calipers, you'll find that braking on curves requires a special technique. It's an especially important one if you're traveling fast or traveling down a hill.

On approaching a curve, always brake before you enter it. Well ahead of time, drop to a speed that you know will see you safely through. Never delay until you're in the curve itself before braking. All sorts of things—none of them nice—can happen if you wait.

For one, you'll be leaning to the side while in the curve. A braking action at that time can cause the bike to slide out from under you and go down flat on the pavement. This is particularly dangerous if you're on a gravel surface.

For another, the curve may be sharper than you had anticipated. You won't be able to brake in time to keep from veering into the opposite lane—and, as luck might have it, right into the path of an approaching car.

To be completely safe, you should enter a curve at a slow speed that causes you to begin pedaling to pick up your pace. Granted, it's not as much fun as sailing through at full tilt. But at least you'll have the fun of getting home all in one piece.

Handling the Gears

Though the gears are meant to make life easier for you, they won't do so unless you know how to shift them correctly. At best, they'll simply refuse to change if shifted in the wrong way. At worst, something in the bike may break.

It's a snap to change gears on a three-speed bike. They're usually shifted by turning the handlegrips to the needed position. All you need do is shift while coasting or standing still. Just remember that three-speed gears won't respond if you attempt to shift while pedaling.

Shifting, of course, is more complex on a ten-speed bicycle because you're working with a greater number of gears. Furthermore, you're dealing with the derailleur system.

Just what is the derailleur system? If you look at a ten-speed bike, you'll see a cluster of small gear sprockets attached to the hub of the rear wheel. They're known as the freewheel sprockets. Usually five in number, they vary in diameter and form a cone there on the hub, with the smallest ones placed on the outside. Up ahead, alongside the pedals, are two larger gear sprockets called the chainwheels. They, too, differ in size and are placed side by side,

DERAILLEUR SYSTEM

with the smaller one on the inside. The job of the derailleur is to give you ten different gears by pushing the bicycle chain from one set of sprockets to another on the freewheel cluster and the chainwheels.

The system was invented in the late nineteenth century by a European cyclist named Paul de Vivie after he had struggled up one hill too many with a bulky one-speed bike. The word *derailleur* comes from the French and means "to derail." This device "derails" the chain and moves it to another place.

The cyclist uses two levers to operate the derailleur system. They're located on either side of the

DERAILLEUR LEVERS

down tube, which runs from the head tube to the base of the bike. Like the caliper brake levers, they trigger the derailleur system by means of cables, with one extending to the rear wheel and the other to the chainwheels. On most ten-speed bikes, as you sit facing forward, the lever on your right moves the chain from one sprocket to the other on the rear wheel, with the left lever handling the chainwheel movements. An adjustment of the lever in one direction sends the chain upward to a larger sprocket. The flick in the opposite direction brings it downward.

Once you acquire the knack of working the system, you should find that shifting causes you no problems. You'll need to remember several points at all times, however. First, never forget that the derailleur won't work unless the pedals are turning. This means that ten-speed shifting is exactly opposite to three-speed shifting. Always change gears while pedaling. A shift while standing still or coasting can jam and damage the gears.

Second, since the pedals must be turning, you must remember that there will be times when you'll have to shift *before* the moment when the new gear is actually needed. Suppose that you're in high gear as you approach an intersection. You know that you must brake to a stop, and you know that you're going to need a lower gear when it's time to move again. Don't wait until you're at a full stop and then snap your fingers and mumble, "Oh, yes. I need a new gear." Shift before you begin coasting to the stop. Don't forget that those pedals must be turning.

You must also remember to shift ahead of time on hills. Let's say that you're heading up an incline. The bike is slowing and you're beginning to pump too hard for comfort. You decide to shift, only to have the derailleurs refuse to cooperate because they're unable to work when there is a heavy pressure on the pedals. And so you must be sure to shift while still pedaling easily. Otherwise, you'll have to reduce the pedal pressure before doing so. The bike will then slow even more and perhaps come to a stop while you're working the levers.

The best way to handle a hill is to study it thoroughly as you approach on the flat. Figure out the gear that you will need to get you comfortably up to the crown (this will come easily with experience). Then shift to the desired gear just before you start to climb.

Whenever you change gears, you'll need to use your ears. They'll tell you whether you've made a clean shift. When the chain slips quietly into place on the new sprocket, all is well. But if you hear a noise of some sort, you've got some more work to do. Noise means that the chain is trying to stay where it is or is attempting to slip into a gear other than the one you want.

A slight adjustment of one of the gear levers is usually all that's needed to right matters. When you hear a clicking or whirring sound behind you, adjust the lever that controls the rear derailleur. A sound underfoot means that an adjustment of the front lever is needed.

One last note: each gear is determined by the number of teeth being used in the front and rear sprockets. Since sprockets can be manufactured with many different numbers of teeth, a wide range of gears is possible—far more than the total used on ten- and fifteen-speed bikes. When you're ready to buy a ten-speed, you may wonder which gears within this wide range will serve you best. There's no need to worry. Just talk to the sales clerk about the kind of riding you plan to do. Explain, for instance, that you live in hilly country and will be spending much of your time working up one slope after another. The sales clerk can use this information, along with a look at your size, to recommend the most suitable gears. More often than not, the gears that come from the factory with the bike will be just fine. If not, you can buy other sprockets as replacements.

RIDING POSITIONS

You should always try to find a comfortable riding position. As we said earlier, you'll be most comfortable if you make certain that your bike fits you and if you then ride leaning slightly forward. Of course, you'll need to shift your position now and again to relieve the stiffness and numbness that can come from sitting too long in just one way.

If you own a ten-speed bike, you are fortunate as

far as riding positions are concerned. The bike enables you to take three different and distinct positions. You'll not only prevent stiffness by shifting from one to another as you ride, but you'll be able to pedal through various kinds of terrain. These three positions are made possible by the shape of the bike's handlebars—a shape, you'll remember, that resembles the horns of a ram.

To begin, you can ride with your hands on top of the bars (Picture A). You're sitting up and leaning a bit forward. Almost upright, you're bound to create some wind resistance for yourself. But you're also in a position that allows your leg and back muscles to work strongly. The position is a good choice when riding along in leisurely fashion on a flat road.

Or you can go to the opposite extreme (Picture B) and drop your hands to the "hooks"—the lower sweep of the ram's horns. Now, bent far over in the position taken by racers, you're reducing wind resistance to a minimum. Also, bent far over, you're able to work your back, arm, leg, and stomach muscles at full power. But there's a disadvantage: you must raise your head sharply to see the road ahead and, unless you're accustomed to the position through long training, you can quickly tire your neck muscles. The "hooks" position is best reserved for short bursts of speed and for hill climbing.

Finally, there's an in-between position (Picture C). It's called "riding the brakes," because you're leaning forward with your hands on the padded

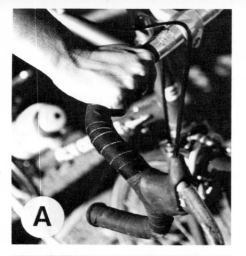

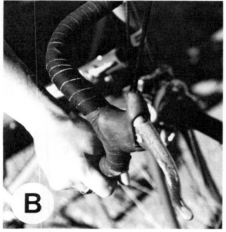

TEN-SPEED RIDING
POSITIONS

brake hoods. You're bent farther forward than when holding the tops of the bars, and so you're reducing wind resistance. At the same time, you're giving yourself good leverage for pedaling. And you're in good shape to use the brakes quickly because your hands are right at the levers. In all, this position is considered the best for long-distance riding and is the one that should be used most of the time. It's the favorite of practically all tourers.

There's a fourth position that you'll need to use at times. As you climb a hill, you may find the slope so steep that, even in a low gear, you must rise from the seat and gain extra power by pumping while standing on the pedals. This is best done by putting your hands on top of the handlebars and then rising so that you come forward and bring your chest above the bars. The position is a comfortable one that gives your legs much added power. And, though standing, you're still able to control the bike with ease.

You can stand in the same way on a three- or one-speed bike if the handlebars are the narrow type. Don't try it on any bike with wide bars, however. When gripping the tops of the bars, your hands are quite close together. The wide bars, sweeping far out to the sides, are then hard to control.

If you're riding a wide-barred bike, always avoid a mistake made by many beginners. Holding the grips, some new cyclists rise straight up and then lean back in the hope of getting more power. Leaning back does nothing but defeat their purpose by causing their bodies to pull against the forward motion of the bike. It's always better to angle forward.

Pumping while standing uses up a great deal of energy. The smart thing to do is stand and pump only for as long as it takes to get the bike back up to speed. Then sit and pedal as usual, rising again only when necessary. Incidentally, many cyclists use the standing pump as a way to shift position from time to time and give their bottoms a few moments of welcome rest from the saddle.

Before ending this chapter, we might as well cover one point about hill climbing that has nothing to do with your riding position. At times, you're going to encounter hills too steep for even the lowest of your gears. You may then find yourself weaving back and forth across the road in an effort to keep the bike moving. This is an obviously dangerous practice because it puts you into the path of passing traffic. Also, struggling as you are, you're using up too much valuable energy.

There's just one smart thing to do: admit that the hill is a bit too tough for you, get off your bike, and push it the rest of the way. It's foolish to play games with traffic. And it's foolish to wear yourself out.

So off you should get. And off you should get without feeling embarrassed. Just remember that there isn't a cyclist around who hasn't walked the bike up a hill at one time or another. Keep on touring and keep on building your strength. You'll come out the winner one day.

GOOD RIDING TECHNIQUES will enable you to pedal along efficiently and for long distances without becoming exhausted. But the mention of playing games with traffic brings us to yet another technique. It's the technique of riding safely, and it's so important that it's going to need some chapters all to itself.

CHAPTER 5

Safe Touring

WE HAVE TO face a fact. Cycling can be a dangerous sport. You're out there on the road with all those cars and trucks. And, riding along on two slender wheels, you must realize that there's always the possibility of a tumble. But all sports have their dangers. You needn't run any greater risk of harm than a baseball or basketball player if you use your head and ride with due caution.

You're bound for an accident or a bad spill, however, if you don't use your head and if you don't follow some common-sense safety rules. In this chapter and the next two, we're going to look at the rules followed by all experienced cyclists. They'll serve you well, whether you're touring or pedaling to school or the grocery store.

Your tours will take you over all sorts of road-ways. You're going to find yourself pedaling along everything from deserted country lanes to crowded city streets—sometimes in the same day. Each type of roadway calls for the use of its own safety rules. But, before we turn to them, let's look at some general rules that apply everywhere.

ON ALL ROADS

Wherever you ride, please remember that you're just like the drivers of trucks or passenger cars: you're operating a vehicle. The laws that apply to other drivers also apply to you. You must, for instance, always have your vehicle under full control. You must obey the traffic signals and observe the rights of pedestrians. If you fail to observe the rules that all vehicle operators must heed, you're headed for an accident—or for trouble with the police.

Along with the motorist, you should always ride on the right side of the road, traveling *with* the flow of traffic, *not against* it. This may come as a surprise if, like too many other cyclists, you feel safer when the cars are coming toward you so that you can see them. Actually, you're safer moving with the traffic.

You have more time to avoid an accident if trouble suddenly looms ahead. Suppose you're traveling

RIDING WITH THE FLOW OF TRAFFIC

to the rear of a car that is in the lane next to yours. The car goes out of control and veers into your path. You have an extra split second to take evasive action because the two of you are moving in the same direction; that extra split second may be all you need to save your life. But imagine that you're traveling against traffic when the car jumps into your lane. You're headed for each other. Gone is the extra time for evasive action.

In addition to traveling with the flow, you should always observe the following seven rules that apply to all vehicle operators:

1. Because yours is a slow-moving vehicle, ride in the right-hand lane, and stay as far to the right

in that lane as you safely can. You will be tempted to move into the middle of the lane, or into the middle of the road if you're out in the country. This isn't a good idea, even if you haven't seen any traffic for an hour or so. Cars can come up from the rear pretty fast. And, obviously, it's deadly to ride in the middle of a winding country road full of blind curves.

2. Ride in a straight line. No weaving through city traffic, please. No swinging from one side of the lane to the other. And no sudden lane changes. Unless you're *very, very* lucky, weaving back and forth is a sure way to win you a trip to the hospital.

3. Always look to the rear and make sure you have a clear path before you change lanes. A glance over your shoulder will do it. It bothers some cyclists to glance over their shoulders during their first days of riding. A little practice will put you at ease. Or you might attach a rearview mirror to your handlebars. Always make certain that it's properly adjusted before you pedal away from home. You can also buy a small rearview mirror that can be attached to your sunglasses.

4. Always use a hand signal before you turn. In most states, the hand signals for cyclists are the same as those for motorists: arm straight up at the elbow for a right turn, straight out for a left turn, and out and down for a stop. Make the signals with your left hand while your right hand remains on the handlebar and guides the bike. Signal well in advance and then return your left hand to the handlebar as you enter the turn.

5. Know and observe the rules of right of way. As a cyclist you don't have the right to slow the normal flow of traffic. If you find cars backing up into a parade behind you on a narrow road, pull off and allow them to pass. At intersections, the vehicles coming from the right are entitled to cross first unless lights or signals say otherwise. And those "yield" signs at corners apply to you as well as to the motorist.

6. Always give pedestrians the right of way. Unless local laws allow you to do so, you may not ride on the sidewalk. And, even if the law allows sidewalk riding, never go whizzing and weaving among crowds of pedestrians. If the sidewalk is at all crowded, do everyone a favor: get off your bike and push it for a while.

7. Never ride at night without a headlamp and a reflector. Actually, these are the minimum items of equipment needed for the dark hours. You can add much other gear for safety. We'll be talking more about night riding later in this chapter.

ESPECIALLY FOR CYCLISTS

In addition to the basic laws that apply to all vehicle operators, a number of rules apply specifically to cyclists. They're to be found in the laws of most states. Even if they're not written into the law in your area, you should still observe them.

For one, never carry any gear or a passenger in

such a way as to block your vision. The laws in many areas prohibit you from carrying someone on your handlebars.

For another, never alter your bike in any manner that makes it less stable or harder to control. Some areas have laws against handlebars with grips that are above the head. Some areas require that the pedals, when in the down position, be no more than a foot off the ground. This is a move against such odd bikes as the old-fashioned "penny-farthing," on which the seat is five or six feet above the ground. Riding a penny-farthing is much like walking on stilts.

Furthermore, you should do no trick riding or stunting—including pedaling without using your hands—on any roadway. If you must risk your neck with stunts, save them for an area reserved for such antics.

Unless you're signaling, you should keep both hands on the handlebars at all times. Not only do you then have the bike under the best control but, if you're working with calipers, you're always just an instant away from the brake levers.

And, finally, stay off freeways, turnpikes, and all other roads where local law prohibits bike traffic. Before leaving on any tour, be sure to check the cycling laws of the areas through which you'll be passing. Learn where you can and cannot take your bike. To repeat a point made in Chapter 3, a call to the local police, the state troopers, or the highway patrol will get you all the necessary information.

NIGHT RIDING

As you know, you should avoid riding at night unless you're a very experienced cyclist. And let's face it. Even if you've been pedaling around for years, it's still best to give yourself and your bike a rest once the sun goes down. For everyone, night riding is just too dangerous.

But there may be times when you must ride in the dark. Then you must be certain that your bike is equipped with a rear reflector and a headlamp. Try to have the best headlamp you can find and the strongest reflector possible.

A reflector and headlamp are the minimum items demanded by the law. Quite sensibly, a number of cities and states now require that you carry additional safety equipment. You should check the local police to learn the requirements in your hometown and in the areas through which you'll be touring.

Even if the local laws call for nothing more than the reflector and headlamp, you'll be wise to think about investing in some useful extras. You can choose from a goodly number on today's cycling market.

For instance, you might want to think about an especially strong headlamp because the ordinary battery-operated ones are of little real value. They enable an approaching motorist to see you, but they don't give you a good look at all the road hazards— everything from chuckholes to broken glass—that may lie in your path. You'll be wise to check into the strobe light favored by so many boaters. About the size of a cigarette pack, it throws a light that is visible from two to five miles and can be purchased at any yachting supply store. But there's a problem. The strobe has a pretty healthy price tag. As this book is being written, the light costs upwards of $50.

Quite helpful also is the armband light. First used in France, it's a small flashlight that, as its name indicates, can be strapped to your arm. It comes with a bulb and two lenses. One lens is red and faces to the rear. The other is clear and faces forward. The red lens continues to serve as a reflector should the bulb happen to burn out. The rig costs just a few dollars, usually between five and ten.

It's a good idea to strap the light to your leg rather than to your arm. Set it in place just below your knee. Then the light will attract more attention as it rises and falls with your every pedaling stroke.

Still another helpful item is reflector tape. Why not place a strip on the back of each pedal? Again, you'll attract attention as it moves up and down. Many cyclists place it in strips along their wheel rims. Others attach a strip to the back edge of their luggage racks. Some wrap it around their handle grips. And some fashion the strips into a triangle on the back of a windbreaker.

So far as clothing is concerned, you might want to think about a Day-Glo vest, which has reflecting material sewn on it. The vest provides fine visibility not only at night but also during daylight hours. It can be purchased for around $20.

Now let's say that you're well equipped with safety devices and that you must ride at night. Here are a few tips meant to help you along your way.

First, when on tour, try to ride only on those nights when the moon is full. Remember, every extra degree of visibility is going to help.

Second, always pedal more slowly than you would in the daytime. Keep a sharp eye out for road hazards. They come quickly out of the dark and sometimes you can't see them until they're inches away from your front tire. If you're riding ahead of friends, call back a warning to them.

Next, what can you do if a car approaches with blazing headlights that threaten to blind you? Try glancing down at the edge of the road to your right. Close your left eye for the moment that it takes the car to sweep past. Your right eye will show you where you're going while your nose serves as a shade for it. Open your left eye again as soon as the head-lights are no longer a bother.

Now for some notes on passing through a town or city. Try always to choose a route that takes you along streets with the least amount of traffic. And always choose the best-lighted streets you can find. For obvious reasons, never cut through a dark or poorly lighted park, a deserted neighborhood, or any other place where the world's creepy people like to hang out. Keep your eyes wide open, of course, for road hazards and approaching headlights. Be especially alert for the glare of headlights coming from either direction as you approach a blind corner or an intersection.

Though we've been talking here about touring, remember that these tips will serve you quite as well as you ride around your neighborhood. So you really should keep them in mind whenever you swing aboard your bike. And, of course, they should always be topped by that best advice of all: give yourself and your bike a rest at night. Save your pedaling for the daylight hours.

Right?

Right.

A FINAL TIP FOR DAY AND NIGHT

I hope that this book contains as many safety suggestions as you'll ever need. But you shouldn't depend on it alone. Rather, you'll be more than wise to see if there's a good bicycle safety program in your area. If so, don't waste a moment in taking advantage of it. Attend the classes. Participate in the riding exercises. Ask questions. Be on hand for all the tests. You're certain to pick up many a vital point that had to be skipped in a book, because no book has all the space in the world. And you're sure to gain some excellent riding experience.

But just where can you find a good safety program in your area? For a start, try your school system. Or see if the Boy or Girl Scouts have a program in which you can participate. Another good possibil-

Bicycles are useful for short or long trips. (**PHOTO COURTESY SCHWINN SALES, INC.**)

ity is your local police department. Police organizations everywhere have long conducted safety clinics, courses, and demonstrations. And don't forget the local bicycle club. Club cyclists are constantly talking safety, and they'll be glad to share with you all that they know. Furthermore, many clubs have safety films and literature for their members and the public.

You can also obtain safety material from national organizations. For instance, the National Safety Council has produced a training course called "All about Bikes." The council makes it available to schools for a small fee per pupil. Why not talk to your principal about securing the course for your class? The principal can obtain information by writing to the council at 425 Michigan Avenue, Chicago, Illinois 60611.

The state offices of the American Automobile Association have material available on safety and bike training; it can be yours if you drop by or write to the AAA office near your home.

As WE SAID right at the beginning of the chapter, your tours are going to take you over country roads and along crowded city streets, sometimes all in the same day. You need to use special safety techniques in the country, and other special methods in the city. In the next chapters, we're going to look at each kind.

Let's start by pedaling along a country road.

CHAPTER 6

Safe Touring on Country Roads

YOU'RE SURE TO love country roads. There you are, out in the open with all that great scenery around you. The air is clean and clear. The scent of trees and flowers and mown fields is everywhere. Now and again, you will see a deer or a herd of grazing horses. And, unlike the crowded city street, the country road carries few cars to pester you and set your nerves on edge.

BUT CARS ARE A PROBLEM

Even though they may be few in number, cars and trucks are still a major problem for the country rider.

94

They're a headache because they travel so much faster here than in the city, and because too many drivers are not alert for cyclists—or for anything else. You must never trust them to watch out for you. You're the one who has to do the watching.

It doesn't seem fair. But so what? What counts is that you never get into an argument with a few tons of moving steel. You're bound to be the loser.

To protect yourself, always remember to ride with the flow of traffic and as far to the right as possible. Constantly check your rearview mirror or glance over your shoulder to see what's coming up from behind. Be especially careful when a truck, a recreational vehicle, or a car with a trailer overtakes you. Slow down and, if possible, pull over even farther to the right. Take a good grip on the handlebars. Steer a straight course. You're going to take a strong blast of air when the monster sweeps past. Have your bike under firm control when that blast hits you.

Actually, you should do more than keep an eye open for vehicles coming from the rear. You must also keep your ears open. It's a pain to keep looking back. The fact is that, now and again, you're going to forget to do so. So, as an extra precaution, develop the habit of listening as you pedal. You'll often be able to hear a car approaching from behind or ahead long before it puts in an appearance. This is especially true on winding roads.

Though you must always ride far to the right, try to spend as much time as you can on the pavement. The ride, naturally, will be smoother for you and easier on the bike. Go onto the dirt shoulder, of course, if you must to protect yourself. If you're forced to the shoulder for any length of time, check it closely as you proceed. Should the surface be firm, fairly smooth, and uncluttered, then everything is fine. But, if it's rocky and bumpy, watch out. It can damage your wheels or tires and even pitch you over. Your best decision here is to get off and walk your way past the rough area.

You may read or hear that it's fun to ride two or three abreast when you're with friends or in a cluster when you're with a group. You and your companions can talk to each other and share the joys of the ride. You're then supposed to get into single file when a car comes up from behind. And you're to decide before the ride just how this regrouping is to be done, agreeing on who will pedal to the front and who will drop behind.

It all sounds safe and fine. *But it's not.* Never ride abreast or in a cluster. It's one of the most hazardous things you can do. Just try getting into single file when somebody is streaking toward you at 70 miles an hour and you'll see what I mean. The practice of riding abreast or in a cluster is considered so dangerous that it's being outlawed in a growing number of areas.

You'll be safest if you and your friends always ride in single file. Maintain a distance of about one bike length between riders. Spaced in this manner, the riders coming up from the rear will have time to

CYCLISTS RIDING TWO ABREAST—A DANGER.

stop or take evasive action should someone take a spill.

At all times, you need to be as alert for cars approaching from the opposite direction as for those coming from behind. This is especially true on sharp or blind curves. Pull over far to the right even if you can't hear an engine sound beyond the curve. Motorists often appear without warning and they have the bad habit of cutting through curves too thinly and entering the opposite lane—yours. It's frightening, and deadly, to be too far out in the lane when a witless driver pulls this stunt.

Be sure also to keep a sharp eye out for gravel, stones, and rocks on the roadway as you go through a curve. Very often, curves are cut into hillsides. Rocks and stones are then forever tumbling to the pavement from the slopes above. And watch for chuckholes. They're caused by motorists who speed through the curves and eventually damage the paving.

THE HAZARDS UNDERFOOT

As a matter of fact, at all times on a country road, you need to watch for rocks and chuckholes, plus an endless assortment of other underfoot hazards. Country roads usually aren't as well cared for as city streets. You're bound to keep meeting such obstacles as broken glass, discarded bottles and cans, sticks and tree branches, garbage, and even car parts. As you enjoy the surroundings, always check the near and middle distance for hazards. If you're speeding along at full tilt, your glance should include the far distance. Regardless of your speed, slow down and pass any obstacle with due caution. If you're with friends, warn them of it.

One obstacle needs special mention: cattle guards. These are groups of metal rails that stretch across the roadway with narrow spaces between them. Cross them at a steady, controlled speed, making certain that you keep your wheels perpendicular to the rails. Don't ever try to cross them at an angle. A wheel can then easily drop between the rails.

Another hazard is fresh blacktop. It's just about the worst substance that anyone has ever created for gumming a bicycle's tires and rims. When you see a patch coming up, try to get off the road and avoid it altogether, even if you have to dismount and push the bike past. You'll lose a few minutes' time, yes. But you won't have to bother with sticky tires later on.

Possibly the biggest hazard of all is the one that sounds like the most fun—the long downhill run. Here's a chance to go whipping along with the wind in your face as you let gravity take over and add wonders to your speed. But wait a minute! Any experienced cyclist will tell you that a fast trip down a hill is the sign of the biking bush leaguer. Disaster can crop up underfoot anywhere along the line.

As a case in point, let me tell you about a friend of mine. Even though she had cycled enough to know better, she took off at full clip down a steep hill. Midway down, she hit a patch of gravel. Her bike went out of control. The front wheel turned sharply to one side, and over the handlebars my friend went. She landed on the stones, with her chin leading. She had a dimple in her chin when she left the top of the hill. Now she has another—a triangular scar.

THOSE LONG, STEEP HILLS

An old cycling adage says, "You can't go up a hill too fast or down one too slow." It's a saying that you should never forget. It will save you many an unnecessary and painful spill. Always treat a downhill run with caution—plenty of it.

As soon as a hill falls away below you, pull over and stop. Take a moment for a careful study of what lies ahead. Do you see any road hazards, such as loose branches or litter, that threaten trouble? Can you pick out patches of loose gravel or car oil? How about chuckholes? Are there curves that promise to be too sharp? All in all, get as acquainted as possible with the road so that you'll be ready for any danger lying in your path.

Next, spend another moment checking your bike and seeing that everything is in proper working order. Take an especially close look at your brakes. If they're calipers, make certain that the pads will touch the wheel rims and not the tires. You're going to be using the brakes quite a bit in the next moments; if the pads are touching a tire, they can wear it down quickly (in Chapter 10 we'll see how to adjust the pads and put them in line with the rims). And check your dunnage to see that it's still securely packed. You don't want anything flying off—or, worse yet, shifting about and giving you a balance problem. If anything has come at all loose, tighten it.

Should you be cycling with friends or a group, don't let everyone go down together. Send them down one at a time or in very small units. Let them start at intervals of perhaps a minute or so. This will keep the bikes from bunching up on the descent. A single mishap can be bad enough if it happens. In a bunched group, it can be disastrous.

It's best, too, to let an experienced cyclist go down first and set a safe pace for the riders who follow. And another experienced cyclist should bring up the rear and come to the aid of anyone who runs into trouble.

Finally, if you're wearing a hat or a cap, pull it down firmly on your head. It's a bore to have to climb back up the hill and search through the roadside bushes for some cherished headgear that flew off midway down the run. If you have regular glasses or sunglasses stowed away in your luggage, put them on. They'll protect your eyes from the wind, flying dust and grit, and, worst of all, flying insects that don't manage to get out of your way.

As you go down the hill, travel at a steady, sensible rate that keeps the bike under control and allows you ample time to sight and avoid obstacles. You'll need to apply your brakes. Try a continual flexing of your fingers on the levers rather than an unrelenting pressure. Unending pressure on caliper brakes causes the rims to become glazed—slicked over with heat—and reduces the gripping power of the pads. Heated rims can also lead to a blown tire. So try the flexing action with your hands, applying just enough pressure to keep the bike under control.

You can use this same flexing action—with your feet—if your bike has coaster brakes. Just as it does with calipers, a steady and hard pressure can overheat the coasters and wear them down.

If your brakes begin to act up, take no chances with them. Don't risk continuing to the bottom of the hill before looking to see what's wrong. Check them immediately. Carefully come to a stop and pull off the road to clear a path for the riders behind you. Very often, you'll find that a simple adjustment of the cable is all that's needed to correct matters. Often, the problem will disappear after the brakes have been given a little time to cool. If the problem can't be righted, walk the bike the rest of the way down.

Finally, remember the art of traveling through curves. Brake before you enter the curve. Be sure that your inside pedal is up as you travel through. The bike will lean to one side. Should the inside pedal be down and should it scrape against the ground—well, you'll be a long time forgetting the experience.

The Animal Problem

Whether riding in the country or the city, you can count on meeting some animals now and again. As they do for the motorist, they can cause you problems by darting or lumbering into your path or giving chase as you pedal past.

You'll, of course, meet more animals in the country than in the city—everything from deer and raccoons and squirrels to cows that have broken out of a field and are wandering along the road. Should you sight an animal on or alongside the road, the first rule for a safe encounter is not to become flustered. Ride slowly past. Give the creature as wide a berth as possible. Be particularly alert for any sudden movements on his part. Deer require special attention. They can bolt in any direction at any time—and without an instant of warning.

Cats and dogs are the animals you will encounter most often. Cats usually present just one problem. There's something in them that makes them enjoy lurking at the roadside as danger—in this case, you—approaches. Then, when you're right on top of them, they take it into their heads to streak across your path. Just pedal slowly and carefully and be ready for that sudden last-minute streak. You'll be okay.

But dogs! Ah yes, dogs! Barking, snapping, and chasing, they're the greatest problem of all. They can —and certainly will, at one time or another—give you some breathless moments. As a friend of mine says, "A dog may be man's best friend. But not when you're on a bicycle."

But, like all problems, a troublesome dog can be handled in a number of ways. I have to admit right at the start, though, that not one of the ways is fool-proof. But, at least, they'll afford you some protection and may help you through a few sticky situations.

First, on sighting a dog that promises to be troublesome, don't panic. Watch to see if you can guess what he has in mind. Does he seem ready to give chase, launch a head-on attack, or just stand there and bark? Pedal steadily and calmly past (at least, have an outward look of calm), and seem to ignore him. As with all animals, give him a wide berth. Quite often, a dog will be a threat only because you're near or passing through territory that he considers his own. If you stay well clear and pedal steadily out of his domain, he'll probably forget about you.

Should the dog come at you, you have several options. First, you can try to outrun him. The success of this tactic depends on your strength, the dog's size, and the condition of the road. Many dogs give up a chase after just a few moments or after you're out of their territory. But it's up to you as to whether you wish to stage a race.

Before the chase starts, you may be able to solve

the problem by startling him off with a firm shake of the finger and an even firmer command to stop. Follow it with a soothing voice and a few kind words and perhaps you'll help matters some more.

Incidentally, if you find yourself coming up behind a dog, call out sharply and firmly. There's a good chance that you'll startle him off. Don't cycle up silently until you're right on top of him. Then he'll be startled in the wrong way.

Now for one major caution: if you do manage to stop an oncoming dog, don't pause and try to make friends. Above all, don't try to pet him. You know nothing about his temperament and, even though he's decided not to attack, he may nip your outstretched hand. A dog bite, even a nip, is no fun at any time, and especially no fun out in the country. You not only have to take care of the injury but you then have to go to the trouble of locating the dog's owner to see if your "friend" has received all the shots necessary to keep you safe from illness. And, all the while that you're looking for the owner, the dog can be at your heels and giving you a bad time. So, even if you seem about to become the greatest of pals, keep your distance. Pedal away and get him out of your life as soon as you can.

If the dog can't be stopped or if he seems to be the sure winner in a race, you probably have no other choice but to climb off your bike before he knocks you down. Dismount on the far side, hold the bike between the two of you, and let him bite the frame,

CYCLIST WALKING BIKE PAST DOG

the luggage rack, or the wheels if he wishes as you walk past. Sooner or later, he'll tire of the fun—hopefully, sooner.

You may also carry a "weapon" or two to help yourself. Many cyclists like the chemical repellent used by postmen, though I've seen a few dogs that it hasn't bothered a bit. Lemon juice or household ammonia in a plastic squeeze bottle is an inexpensive repellent. If you're willing to spend the money, an electric cattle prod can be a good deterrent. You might pick up a slender switch from the roadside and carry it with you. Or bring along a supply of dog biscuits to strew in your attacker's path as he comes at you.

Perhaps your best choice is the bicycle pump that can be attached to the bike frame. It's a sturdy object that's always within easy reach. But, whenever using it or any other sticklike weapon, try to do no more than wave it in front of the dog's nose, letting him bite it rather than you. It's dangerous to whack the animal because you'll likely succeed only in angering him more. If you do have to hit him, don't strike out blindly. Do what you can to take careful aim. And try, as a friend of mine advises, to rap him across the nose. My friend says that a knock on the nose will often take the fight out of the most threatening of dogs.

Two final points. First, if you see a dog that promises to be downright dangerous, don't be embarrassed about becoming a coward. Turn your bike around and travel in the opposite direction before trouble starts. Try to figure another way around that yapping obstacle. Or wait until he disappears.

Second, don't let the threat of dogs discourage you. You're bound to meet them at one time or another, and they've turned many a beginner off about cycling. But you're bound to encounter them only on occasion, with most of them being friendly creatures. So don't let them keep you from participating in a highly enjoyable sport. Just know that they're there and have to be handled—calmly and firmly.

CHAPTER 7

Safe Touring on City Streets

IT WOULD BE nice if you could do an entire tour without once having to face all the problems and all the four-wheel mechanical monsters that are to be found on city streets. But that's just about out of the question. Your tour may have to start in town. And it's almost sure to take you through a town at one point or another along the way.

The city street has all the obstacles that you'll find on a country road—everything from litter and car parts to chuckholes and patches of gravel. On top of all else, it has some special hazards distinctly its own. You have to keep on watch for open manholes, storm drains, and broken gutters. And don't forget about streetcar tracks. They're constant threats, because they can cause skids or trap your wheels and throw you over.

And so you need to be as observant in town as on a country road. Ride attentively and carefully. Ride with your eyes to the front, checking the middle and near distance. Always.

CARS, CARS, AND MORE CARS

Cars and trucks, of course, are your biggest headache. They're everywhere, rushing here and there, and your best bet is to remain just as far away from them as possible. Stay well to the right in the curbside lane. And observe all the basic rules of safe riding: no weaving through traffic, no floating from one side of the lane to the other, no flying across intersections, no turning without a hand signal, and no riding on the sidewalk (even if local laws permit it). Above all, never challenge a car by trying to beat it to a turn— or to anything else. Remember, if anything goes wrong, you're sure to be the loser.

As you pedal in the curbside lane, you'll need to be aware of the cars to both sides—those that are moving and those that are parked. Your job is to steer a path that will carry you safely between them, as distant from each as you can manage. Here are some tips that will help you along.

First, let's talk about the moving cars. You'll need to keep checking their positions, and you'll most likely have to do so by glancing into your rearview mirror or over your shoulder. The noise of city traffic usually makes it difficult, if not impossible, to hear cars coming up behind you. If you're without a mirror, learn to glance over your left shoulder without veering off course; a little practice in an open area will do wonders here. Your glance should take no more than a split second. Then it's back to looking ahead again.

Now let's consider the parked cars. They may seem perfectly harmless sitting there at the curb. But don't be fooled. They can give you some bad moments if you're not alert. As you pass each one, look to the next ones in line. Is there someone up ahead

PARKED CAR DOOR OPENING IN CYCLIST'S PATH

who has just backed into a parking space? Don't put it past that driver to open the door and step out into your path just as you're drawing alongside. Do you see exhaust coming from a tailpipe? That can tip you off that a driver has just fired up the engine and is getting ready to pull away from the curb. And while we're on the subject of sudden pullouts, take care when you come abreast of a line of cars behind a stalled vehicle in the middle of the street. An impatient driver somewhere in the line is likely to decide to swing out and get past—by jumping into your lane.

As you're watching the parked cars, it's a good idea to develop the habit of glancing down at their front wheels. Children are famous for stepping between curbside vehicles and then darting out into traffic. Small as the youngsters are, their heads often don't show above the hood. But a glance at the front wheel may show you the tips of two little, impatient feet.

You can easily see adult pedestrians, of course, as they step between cars before starting across a street. But don't trust them to see you. If they're looking somewhere else and seem at all ready to take off, get ready to apply your brakes. Call a warning, if necessary. Call in a voice that they can hear, but speak as gently as possible. Pedestrians are more accustomed to cars than to bicycles. A rough shout and the sight of a bike swishing toward them can fluster pedestrians—with unexpected and unhappy results.

All this sounds as if drivers and pedestrians are

not required to keep an eye out for you. They're supposed to watch for cyclists and exercise due caution because you have as much right to be on the street as they. But the sad fact is that they often forget that you're around. Worse yet, some drivers think that the city streets are for them alone. Impatient with all the traffic around them, they grow unduly angry at the sight of a bicycle. Thanks to the anger, all caution and good sense go out the window.

So, as we said at the start of Chapter 6, you must never depend on others to watch for you. You have to do the watching. As unfair as it is, it's the only way to guarantee your safety.

The need to ride as far to the right as possible may bring you up against some curbside problems. You know how much debris is to be found in any gutter. And you know that, sooner or later, you're going to encounter one of those storm-drain grates into which your wheels can so easily drop. Many of these cycling headaches can be handled without too much difficulty if you pedal attentively. But sometimes there will be so much litter that your bike begins to bounce wildly. If traffic is light, you can move out to the smoother surface of the lane; just be sure that you first check for cars behind you and that you angle gradually rather than jump suddenly outward. But, if traffic is at all heavy out there, it's best not to challenge the cars. You'll be safer to dismount and push your bike along the sidewalk for a few minutes.

Driveways and alleys also need their share of

attention. Watch for cars that may come barging out of them. Alleys that open onto streets from between buildings or from behind hedges are particular hazards. Always reduce speed as you approach. Listen for the sound of a car. Watch for the sudden glint of a bumper or a headlight. Then, when you're sure that all is well, across you go.

INTERSECTION FACTS

Of course, you know better than to fly across an intersection or to try beating a traffic light. But there are some other "intersection facts" that you should know about. First, when stopped at an intersection, behave as thoughtful motorists do. Never let yourself come to a stop in the middle of a crosswalk so that the pedestrians have to work their way around you. That sort of thing annoys them—as it should, because the crosswalk is rightfully theirs—and you can give all cyclists a bad name as you stand there and make life momentarily difficult for shoppers with their arms full of parcels. You'll do a nice public relations job for cyclists everywhere if you stop at the edge of the crosswalk and allow the people on foot to have free passage.

Need it be said that you should always stop at the *inside* edge? A stop beyond the crosswalk may leave the pedestrians free—but there you are with your nose sticking out into the path of the cars crossing the intersection from your left.

BIKES STOPPED PROPERLY AT CROSSWALK

Second, as you approach an intersection, be aware of the cars behind you. There's always the chance that some car will pass you and then cut across your front to make a right turn. You may be up against some impatient soul. More likely, you're dealing with someone who has failed to see you because he or she is watching for the traffic coming from the left.

Finally, unless you're a very experienced cyclist, it's wisest not to pedal across a busy intersection. You've got cars making turns and throngs of pedestrians, any of whom might wander out of the crosswalk at your side and into your path. Your best bet is to dismount and walk across with them. The same, by the way, is true when you come to a narrow bridge in heavy traffic. There's just too little space for riding comfort.

To END THESE chapters about safety, let me stress again a point I made earlier. When planning your tour, try to find a route that will carry you clear of the downtown district or clear of the town altogether. The safest way to handle a city street, whether you're on tour or on an everyday ride, is to avoid it completely.

CHAPTER 8

Getting Ambitious

NOW THAT YOU'VE tried your first tours, you may be content to continue traveling short distances with one or two friends. If so, fine. You've found a sport that takes just a few hours of your time but gives you a great deal of pleasure and adventure in return. Keep on having fun.

But, on the other hand, you may want to try something more ambitious. Perhaps you'd like to join —or lead—a large group on a day-long tour. Or perhaps you'd like to try a long journey with friends, your family, or a group.

If this is what you have in mind, then this chapter is especially for you. Its purpose is to help you realize your ambitions.

THE GROUP TOUR

The best way to begin touring with a group is to join a bicycle club and participate in its outings. Very quickly, you'll learn the ropes of handling a large number of cyclists. In time, you're likely to become one of the group leaders. Once you do, here are some of the things you'll find yourself thinking about.

As you know, when you tour with just one or two friends, it's wisest to pick companions who pretty well equal you in strength and riding skill. The same goes for a group. But it's obvious that hardly any group is going to consist of like cyclists. You're almost certain to get a mixture. Some people will be strong and experienced, and others will be inexperienced and not at all strong.

This mixture needn't be a problem if you plan the trip carefully. Start by dividing the entire party into small units. Place cyclists of similar strength and skill in each unit. Each unit will then be able to proceed at its own best pace. The top cyclists can speed along as swiftly as they wish while the slower ones set a more leisurely pace for themselves. If possible, however, there should be at least one experienced cyclist with each unit to serve as a guide and lend a hand with repairs should there be a breakdown.

With the units traveling at different speeds, the entire group can't help becoming separated. Your next job is to get all the people back together again from time to time. This can be done by planning a series of rest stops at designated points along the way. On reaching the rest stops, the faster cyclists can relax and await the arrival of their slower companions. The entire tour party can then be together for a few moments. The units may take off again at the same time or depart at intervals.

For any tour, you should check the route ahead of time so that, in keeping with that old cycling rule, you never travel along a road that's totally unfamiliar. When you check the route, look for shortcuts here and there. If they are safe, tell the slower cyclists to use them. The shortcuts will help them reach the rest stops—or the final destination—at about the same time as the faster riders. Sometimes, they'll even arrive there before everyone else.

No matter how short the journey, every tour group should have a recognized leader or group of leaders. If you're traveling with a club, it will choose the leader. Should you dream up the trip, you'll probably be expected to act as leader. But you should take on the job only if you have the experience and maturity for it. Otherwise, you should find an experienced cyclist who is willing to serve in your place. Preferably, the leader should be as old as or older than the others in the group.

When you are the leader, you'll be responsible for making all the tour preparations, though you may well have the help of several fellow cyclists. In addition to checking the route ahead of time, you must choose the rest stops. You must see that maps are made and distributed among the units. You will have to be sure that the cyclists are informed of all that lies ahead; they must know of such matters as road conditions, challenging hills, towns to be skirted, and hazards to be avoided. You must be sure that every rider is properly equipped for the day and that each bike is in suitable condition.

Once the tour begins, you and your assistants are responsible for seeing that everyone travels safely, that no one becomes lost, and that the riders are given help whenever there is a breakdown.

As soon as you begin riding with groups, you're going to hear about what's called a "sag wagon." As leader, you may or may not want to put it to use. A sag wagon is a car, a station wagon, a bus, or pickup truck that travels with groups and carries the cyclists' extra equipment or even all their gear. It is also used to transport tired riders and broken bikes the rest of the way to the final destination.

The sag wagon ordinarily moves along slowly at a distance behind the group. The driver may be a volunteer—usually a parent or friend—or the cyclists themselves may take turns at the wheel. Many experienced bikers don't like the idea of a sag wagon, arguing that it reduces the challenge and adventure of the trip. But just as many others think it a nice convenience, especially for groups that include touring newcomers.

The sag wagon can be put to another purpose.

Suppose that your trip is to end with a cookout at a campground. The sag wagon can carry all the food and other supplies. At some point along the way, it can hurry on ahead to the campground. Then the driver, with an assistant or two, can prepare the meal so that it will be ready for the cyclists on their arrival. And you can bet that they're going to be very hungry.

THE LONG TOUR

Most cyclists look on a long tour as a trip that keeps you out at least one or two nights and covers several hundred miles (experienced riders, remember, think nothing of pedaling between a hundred and two hundred miles a day). A tour can take you anywhere and last as long as you wish it to last.

You can head out for a weekend in your immediate area if you wish. You can tour your state with your parents during the family vacation. You can drive to a distant area and begin your tour from there. You can devote weeks, or even months, to a trip across our country or some foreign land. It's up to you as to where you want to go, what you want to do, and how long you want to be on the road. Just let your imagination and your cycling ambitions be your guide.

Regardless of your ambitions, you plan the long tour in exactly the same way as you planned your first jaunts of a few hours. The plans, of course, are more complex because of the greater distance involved. And, being complex, they're twice as much fun to make. You begin, as usual, by choosing your destination.

WHERE TO GO?

If you're planning a long tour in your immediate area, you'll probably be able to pick your own destination and route. You—perhaps with an assist from your parents or friends—know the surroundings well enough to do the job. But, if you're puzzled as to where to go and how to get there, you can turn again to the organizations that helped you with your first trips. The local bicycle club, the police, the parks and recreation department, and the neighborhood bicycle shop will all be able to give you ideas about a destination and an interesting route.

But perhaps you'd like to try a distant area. You can turn for help to the very same organizations in that region. Or you can seek help from a number of national cycling organizations that provide excellent touring information and often sponsor trips of their own. For instance, you can get in touch with these groups:

- *American Youth Hostels, Inc.* As you'll soon learn, AYH offers inexpensive overnight accommodations all across the country for cyclists. It also has handbooks on cycling and maps of tour routes in all parts of the United States. One of the best touring guides around is the *American Youth Hostels' North American Bicycle Tour Atlas.* Written by Warren Asa, AYH's western regional director, the atlas provides easy-to-read maps of 150 different tours. It also contains much information on each of the tours. Information on the atlas and other publications can be had by writing to American Youth Hostels, Inc., National Administrative Office, 1332 I St., N.W., Suite 800, Washington, D.C. 20005, or The Metropolitan New York Council, 132 Spring St., New York, New York 10012.

- *Bikecentennial.* Bikecentennial publishes a variety of helpful materials on tour routes throughout the country. It also publishes a monthly newsletter and *The Cyclists' Yellow Pages*, a list of national cycling associations and state agencies that have touring information. Included also is general information on tour routes, campgrounds, and hostels. Bikecentennial's address is P.O. Box 8308, Missoula, Montana 59807. A nominal fee is charged for membership in Bikecentennial.

- *League of American Wheelmen.* The league was formed in 1880 in Rhode Island and grew to a membership of over 100,000 by the turn of the century. The coming of the automobile caused its membership to dwindle, with the result that the club went out of existence. But it returned to life when cycling became popular again a few years ago. Today, the league is recognized as the grand-daddy of all cycling organizations in our country. It provides information on every type of biking activity, including touring. There is a small fee for membership in the league. The league's address is P.O. Box 988, Baltimore, Maryland 21203.

- *Cyclists' Touring Club.* Founded in 1878 and recognized as the world's oldest nationwide cycling club, this organization can supply you with much information on touring in the United Kingdom and Europe. It publishes a booklet of places where you can board and have breakfast while touring, and it has a service to help you with travel plans. You can write to the club at Cotterell House, 69 Meadow, Godalming, Surrey, England GU7 3HS.

With all the local and national organizations that are ready to lend you a hand with advice, you should have no trouble finding a good tour to a nearby or distant destination. The fact is that practically the whole world is within the reach of the adventuring cyclist.

REACHING YOUR DESTINATION

If you're lucky and have all the time in the world, you can take as long as you please to complete your tour. The chances are, though, that you'll be forced to make the trip in a certain number of days so that you can get back to school or your job. As soon as you've picked your final destination and route, you should divide the tour into daily distances. If the daily distances show that the journey can be made within the allotted time, you're in business. If they don't, you'll need to change your final destination to a spot a little closer to your starting point.

It's not necessary to divide the trip into equal daily distances, nor is it always possible to do so. Base the distances on what you learn from your maps and from all the other information that you collect. You may see that your trip will take you through hilly country on one day and across a flatland the next. A shorter distance should be planned for the "hilly" day. You must also take into account the stops you'll make at parks, historic sites, vista points, and the like. And don't forget that you'll want to end each day's run at a spot that offers overnight accommodations: a motel, a hostel, or a good campsite for your tent.

So plan your daily distances carefully. Try to be sure that you'll be able to complete each day's run in a reasonable length of time.

Once you've decided on the daily distances, it's time to make your route map. You may use either of two kinds of maps. You may decide on a single one for the entire tour, or you may carry a separate map for each day's travel. Though both are fine, many cyclists prefer the separate maps because each one is small and can be conveniently handled. Also, separate maps allow more space for printing in the names and locations of points of interest.

It goes without saying that you should learn the route ahead of time. Since you'll be traveling a great distance—or going to a distant spot to begin the tour—you won't be able to drive over the route beforehand. This makes it imperative for you to collect all the information possible from the many groups that have been mentioned in this chapter. Then, as you're traveling, ask for news as to what lies ahead from local residents and fellow wanderers.

Now for a special point: if your tour is to begin at a point distant from your home, you'll need to plan on how to get your bike to the jumping-off spot. If you plan to go by car with your parents or friends, you'll need a rack for the bikes. You can purchase a rack at any bike shop. They come in models that attach to the rear or the roof of the car. Before making your purchase, tell the sales clerk about the bikes and your car. He or she will then be better able to help you choose a suitable rack.

You may have to travel to your starting point by air. You'll find that most airlines have cardboard boxes for bicycles. Usually, you must dismantle the bike to get it into the carton, removing the wheels, handlebars, pedals, and seat. You may or may not be charged extra for carrying the bike. Much depends on the policy of the airline.

Bikes are also usually permitted aboard trains and buses. Sometimes, a railroad line will allow you to store the bike intact in the baggage car. More often, however, the bike will have to be disassembled and placed in a cardboard box. Packaging the bike in a carton is always necessary on a bus because of the small amount of storage space available. On both trains and buses, you may be expected to supply your own box. You can purchase one at a bike shop. Again, you may or may not have to pay for this extra luggage.

WHERE TO STAY

On the surface, the problem of where to stay each night seems a simple one. The accommodations that the motorist uses are available also to the cyclist. You can stop at a motel, a hotel, a guest house, a friend's home, or, if you're camping, at any spot where you're allowed to pitch a tent.

But suppose that you're not equipped for camping or that your pocketbook can't handle the expense of a hotel or motel. Don't give up hope. You may then be able to take advantage of accommodations that are not open to motorists. These are the accommodations offered by American Youth Hostels, Inc. AYH hostels are simple, clean, and inexpensive shelters meant mostly for people who are traveling under their own power—hiking, cycling, or canoeing.

Hostels, all of them clean and well maintained, are to be found throughout the world. There are more than 4,500 of them in fifty nations. AYH maintains more than a hundred in the United States and can point the way to those outside the country. Canada boasts of at least seventy.

To take advantage of the hostels, you must be a member of AYH. The membership fee is slight. A very inexpensive hosteling pass is available to travelers under eighteen years of age. It enables you to stay overnight in hostels here and in Europe at a charge that ranges from three to five dollars. In most hostels, you must do your own washing and cooking.

Incidentally, you shouldn't be fooled by the word "youth" in AYH's title. Your parents and other adults can also take advantage of the accommodations. The hostels are open to travelers of all ages. The main purpose of the hostels is to help people traveling under their own steam. Though some hostels welcome cars, the priority is given to bikes and hikers, especially during the busy season.

You can obtain all needed information and, once you join, a list of its hostels by writing to AYH at its Washington, D.C., or New York City address.

What to Take

Obviously, you'll need more gear for your long trip than you did for your first short jaunts. But you'll be surprised at how little you'll require as a minimum. And you should always try to keep all gear at a minimum, taking along only what you think you'll actually need. No frills, please. The less you carry, the easier it will be to pedal. Your gear, remember, consists of clothing, repair equipment, and food.

Clothing

In addition to your riding outfit (which, you'll recall, can be either comfortable everyday clothing or a cycling jersey and shorts), you should carry at least two changes of underwear and socks. You can wash your used garments every day or two and hang them out to dry.

Pick out a lightweight outfit for "dress up" at night. It can be as informal as you wish, the main idea being to have something that gets you out of your sweaty riding clothes at day's end. It's really refreshing to have clean clothes to wear for dinner, a dance, a movie, or just a chat around the campfire. Slacks and a shirt are fine for boys while girls will find that a shirt and slacks or a skirt are good choices. Think about a shirt with long sleeves to provide a bit of extra comfort on chilly nights. Jeans, of course, can be substituted for the slacks or skirt.

You'll be happiest if your dress-up outfit is made of a wash-and-wear, wrinkleproof material so that it won't look a mess when you unpack it at day's end.

The dress-up outfit should also include a pair of shoes. You can choose any type you wish just so long as they're suitable for street wear. It will be a good idea, though, to select something with hard rubber soles. Then the shoes can be used as substitutes should your cycling shoes give out.

Round off your dress-up garb with a warm sweater or a windbreaker, either of which you can wear, if need be, as you pedal along. If the weather promises to be a shade too cold, you might think about packing a suit of long underwear.

Finally, for day and night use, put in a water-proof poncho or a rain cape as a safeguard against a shower or downpour. The poncho is a good choice because it can do double duty as a bike cover at night or, if you're camping, as a ground cover. A rain cape flaps less than a poncho as you're pedaling and so may be a more comfortable choice, but it doesn't protect your feet. Avoid one type of foul-weather gear— the oilskin rain suit. Though it's a fine protector, it has a major drawback in that it restricts evaporation. Pretty soon, perspiring as you pedal, you'll be as wet inside the oilskin as you are outside it.

Now what about toilet gear? It should include all the items necessary for washing, cleaning your teeth, and caring for your hair. Boys will find it convenient to use a battery-powered razor for shaving. Girls should carry their makeup and lotions in plastic bags to protect against leakage. In addition to the obvious gear, be sure to take along a first-aid kit, a sewing kit, toilet paper, bath and face towels, a small metal mirror, and insect repellent.

Repair Gear

You'll need the tools necessary to make a variety of roadside repairs, everything from the always-to-be-expected flat tire to a broken chain. As you did on your short tours, you may gather the tools from around the house. Your best bet, though, is to invest in a good and complete tool kit intended for your make of bike. If a repair manual came with the bike (or if you've bought one along the line), find a place for it. Together, the manual and kit should enable you to make all the most common roadside repairs.

In addition to the tool kit, don't forget to take along the following items:

1. A tire-patch kit.
2. A spare tire tube in case you suffer a blowout that can't be repaired. Only one spare is necessary. If you lose both tires, you'll be able to borrow a spare from one of your companions, whose gear should be identical to yours.
3. At least four extra spokes.
4. Two spare brake pads.
5. A rear derailleur cable.
6. A rear brake cable. Remember, both the rear derailleur and brake cables are long enough to serve also as front cables.
7. One or two spare toe-clip straps.
8. A length of extra chain—at least six links long.
9. Above all, remember to include your tire pump.

Food

Food need be no more of a problem on tour than it was on your short jaunts. Unless you're in the most remote areas, you can purchase food at grocery stores along the way. In fact, if you wish and if you have enough money, you can do most of your eating in restaurants.

If you plan to pass through an especially isolated region, you would be wise to carry one or two day's worth of rations; they're comforting to have on hand should you find yourself stuck somewhere. Avoid canned rations, however, because of their weight. And don't store your food in glass containers because of the possibility of breakage. You might take a look at the dehydrated foods displayed in shops for campers and backpackers. They're somewhat expensive, but they're a blessing as far as weight is concerned.

In addition to your rations, you'll need the energy snacks mentioned in Chapter 2. Nibble on them as you pedal. And please remember the other advice given in that chapter: eat lightly during the day, always choosing nutritious foods, and save your heavy meal for the evening.

Packing Your Bike

Any talk of packing your bike for a long tour must begin with the items necessary for storing and carrying your luggage. Basically, you need two types of equipment: racks and carriers.

Racks

Racks, of course, are metal "tables" attached to the bike. At maximum, a bicycle can accept two racks, one over each wheel. The front-wheel rack is several inches shorter than its companion to the rear. Depending on the amount of luggage being carried, you're free to use one or two racks. Should you choose just one, it should be the rear rack. Not only is it a bit larger but, when laden with gear, it sets the center of gravity low over the rear wheel and gives you better balance.

Your present bike may be equipped with what's known as a "student rack." Meant for carrying books and lunches to school, it's a somewhat fragile piece of equipment with usually just one support strut to either side. It isn't really strong enough for the loads and rigors of long-distance travel; you'll be better off if you invest in a regular touring rack.

A good touring rack is made of sturdy aluminum or steel coated with rubber. It usually boasts two or three support struts on either side. The rack is engineered to handle loads from fifteen pounds to around one hundred. Once bolted to the frame, it becomes a solid part of the bike.

At present, a high-quality touring rack costs in the neighborhood of twenty or thirty dollars, but it's a good investment. With care, it will serve for years. Also, it doesn't cost a great deal more than the much weaker student rack, some of which are priced at around ten dollars.

Carriers

Made of cloth, synthetic fabrics, or leather, luggage carriers are the bags in which you carry your gear. Several different types are available, the most popular being the pannier.

The pannier consists of two bags that drape over the rack so that they hang to either side of the wheel. Made for both the front and rear racks, panniers can be found in a variety of price ranges and usually feature such conveniences as zippered compartments and adjustable straps for holding your gear in place.

Since racks are manufactured in several widths, they won't accept every pannier. When buying a pannier, don't take it home before checking to see that it fits your rack. It should drape snugly over the

TOURING RACK

rack and neither hang too low (to the wheel hub is about right) nor flop about. See, too, that the bags don't extend so far forward that your heels strike them as you pedal.

Another tip: make sure that the pannier is reinforced with "stiffeners"—fabric or cardboard liners that strengthen the walls nearest the wheels. They're worth any extra price that you may have to pay. The stiffeners keep the weight of your gear from pushing the walls inward and brushing against the wheel spokes.

And now a caution: there is a type of pannier bag that hangs from the top tube. Unless Aunt Minerva gives you one for Christmas and you simply must use the thing, it's best to avoid it altogether (and even best to lose Aunt Minerva's as soon as possible). When bulging with even the slightest amount of gear, it's going to scrape against your knees, eventually rub them raw, and drive you crazy in the meantime.

If you wish, you may carry a handlebar bag. It may be used along with or in place of a front pannier. Within easy reach as it is, the handlebar bag is great for a camera and film, a lightweight jacket, snacks, or any other items that you'd like right at hand while you ride.

Saddlebags are another possibility for storage. Though they can also be used on long trips, they're especially good for shorter runs if you don't care to go to the expense of a pannier. Depending on the

BICYCLE WITH PANNIER BAG AT REAR

amount of cargo that it's made to carry, a saddlebag may be strapped to the luggage rack or tied to the underside of the seat.

Weight and Balance

When the time comes to pack, you should keep in mind several basic rules. First, your cargo should not outweigh your bike. A bike, along with the tool kit and tire pump, will usually weigh around thirty pounds. You should make every effort to keep your cargo under this weight limit. Cyclists often overload their bikes—a dangerous practice that makes steering and balance difficult.

Next, as you pack, concentrate on keeping the center of gravity low so that the bike will always be stable and well balanced. Place the heaviest items at the bottom of the pannier bags. You can then tuck lightweight pieces around the heavy things and up at the top. If you're carrying a sleeping bag, it will ride nicely on top of the rack.

Again for stability, you should also try to keep the center of gravity toward the middle of the bike. The heaviest items should go toward the front of the rear pannier and toward the rear of the front pannier. And there's no need to warn you against packing the bike more heavily on one side than on the other.

If you use two panniers, you'll further help the

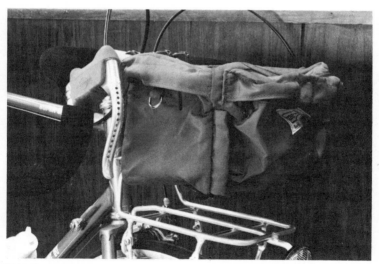

HANDLEBAR BAG

bike's stability by distributing the weight between the bags according to a certain ratio. In general, about two-thirds of the weight should go to the rear pannier, with the remaining one-third reserved for the one up front. The additional weight at the rear will also improve the always-weak traction on the rear wheel.

Suppose that you also have a handlebar bag. As you know, it's great for those items that you want within easy reach. But take care to pack the bag so that it's as light as possible. The handlebar bag is positioned high on the bike and, if heavily laden, will tend to lift the center of gravity.

You should plan to give a fair amount of time to your packing chores. Start with a list that you can check to make certain that you don't forget anything vital. Then experiment until you find the manner in which to pack the gear, not only for balance but also for convenience. Always remember that the better you organize your cargo at the start, the easier it will be to find and keep things in order during the tour.

PREPARING YOUR BIKE

Just as you did before your first short jaunts, you'll need to check the condition of your bike before taking off on a long tour. This time, however, the check will have to be far more thorough than before. Many rigorous miles lie ahead, and your bike must be ready for them.

Let your check run from one end of the bike to the other. Here's what you'll need to do:

1. Check all bearings. Worn bearings should be replaced, lubricated, and adjusted.
2. Look closely at the chainwheels and the rear sprockets. If you find broken or bent teeth on any unit, you must replace it.
3. Look just as closely at the front and rear derailleurs. Adjust them if necessary. If they're at all badly worn, they should be repaired or replaced.
4. Take another close look, this time at the front and rear brake and derailleur cables. If they are worn or damaged, replace them.
5. Check the trueness of both wheels. Make certain that they neither hop nor wobble. Bent and broken spokes need to be replaced.
6. As part of your wheel check, inspect the tires. Are they worn or in any way damaged? If so, replace them.
7. Check the pedals. You should remove them from the bike and spin them with your fingers. If they don't behave properly, you'll need to service or replace the bearings.
8. Test the brakes for their response. Check the brake levers, pads, and calipers. Should any of them reveal excessive wear, make the appropriate replacement.
9. Check the bike chain. If necessary, invest in a new chain.

Many of these jobs will be explained in greater detail in Chapter 10, but it takes a pretty accomplished mechanic to do them all. If you're up to the job, carry on. But, if not, don't hesitate to head for the local bike repair shop. A stem-to-stern check and overhaul will be on the costly side, yes. But it will be well worth the money if it saves you from a serious breakdown at some spot that is about ten miles from nowhere.

A caution. Is your bike brand-new? It is? Then ride it as often as possible in the weeks before the tour. Any new piece of machinery is likely to have "bugs" in it. You should discover and correct them before you risk a long journey. Furthermore, only a scant few bikes handle in exactly the same way, and you're going to need some time to accustom yourself to the steering, pedaling, and brake response. So find those bugs, be rid of them, and get well acquainted with your new bike. Then it will be time for the open road.

PREPARING YOURSELF

If you're to avoid undue tiredness and muscle soreness, you must be physically ready for the tour. Being physically ready means being in fit condition to pedal each daily distance without too much discomfort. It's going to take some training to get you into that shape, even though you've been building your strength with short runs.

Starting one to two months before the tour, take as many short trips as you can. Gradually increase your distances until you're matching—or better yet, exceeding—the daily mileage that you'll be clocking

A bicycle touring helmet—an important piece of safety equipment. (PHOTO COURTESY SCHWINN SALES, INC.)

A compact lantern, handy for camping trips. (PHOTO COURTESY OF L.L. BEAN, INC.)

on your long tour. At the same time, start a program of daily calisthenics. Start slowly and steadily increase the amount of time you spend on the exercises. Concentrate especially on exercises that build your legs and limber your muscles. Round everything off with a proper diet and plenty of sleep. Of course, drugs, alcohol, and cigarettes should have no place in a cyclist's life.

Suppose that you've planned your tour for early spring. It's likely then, that you'll be doing your training in poor weather and won't have the chance for too many short runs. If so, there are rollers on which you can stand your bike indoors and pedal in place. Or you may have a bicycle exerciser at home. In either case, do all the stationary riding you can, concentrating the whole time on hitting a steady pedaling pace.

With just a few weeks of simple training, you'll be as ready to go as your bike. So good luck, and have a great trip.

CHAPTER 9

Bicycle Camping

THOUGH THIS BOOK is called *Bicycle Touring and Camping*, it seems that we haven't mentioned camping too often thus far. Actually, we've been talking about it all along, because everything we've said about touring also applies to camping.

Camping can play a part in your cycling life in any number of ways. When on tour, you may camp out each night to save the expense of eating in restaurants and staying in motels. Or you can design your whole trip around camping, pedaling from one campsite to the next. Or you can spend a few hours traveling to a campground, pitch your tent there, and then return home after a weekend of fishing, hiking, swimming, or just lazing in the sun.

You're in the same position as you are when you tour. You can go wherever you wish—to spots either close to home or far away—just so long as you pick a place where camping is permitted. You can do whatever you wish once you get there. Just let your imagination be your guide.

There is just one basic difference, really, between a straight tour and a camping tour. When camping, you need to store some additional gear aboard your bike. One of the main purposes of this chapter is to talk about that extra gear.

YOUR CAMPING GEAR

When you first start camping, you're almost certain to make one mistake. You're going to heap your bike with far more gear than you really need. But there's no cause for embarrassment. This is a mistake made by practically every would-be Daniel Boone.

On your first expedition, pack your bike as lightly as possible, and then keep track of what you actually use. Next time, leave behind all the things that just "went along for the ride." Over a period of time, as you become more adept at living in the outdoors, you'll probably find yourself getting along with less and less. Carrying unnecessary gadgets and luxuries will be a thing of the past. You'll be down to the essentials of easy travel.

But just what are the essentials?

Sleeping Bag or Bedroll

At the top of the list is a commercially made sleeping bag or a bedroll that you put together yourself. In either case, it should be as comfortable as possible. After a long day at the pedals, you're going to want some restful sleep.

Your bedroll can be a blanket that you wrap around yourself. Or you can make a sleeping bag by folding one or two blankets and sewing them together. But, on two counts, you'll probably be happier with a commercially made sleeping bag: it's better insulated against the nighttime cold than is the blanket, and it's far less bulky and thus easier to pack aboard the bike.

But there's a problem here. A good quality sleeping bag is expensive. In fact, it can be one of the more expensive purchases you'll make as a touring camper. So, if you're trying the outdoor life for the first time and your pocketbook is a bit on the thin side, you might want to follow the suggestion of a friend of mine who advises that you start with a bedroll. Then, should you find that camping really isn't your thing, you won't have invested too much money in it. But, if

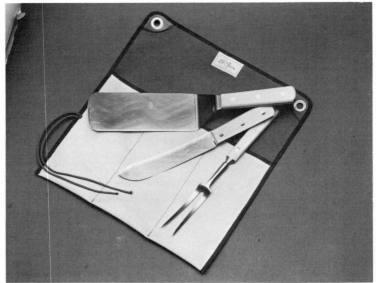

Camping equipment that is light and compact enough to be carried on bicycle trips: portable water bag made of nylon; spatula, butcher knife, and fork for cooking camp meals; battery hand light with wrist lanyard cord; front and rear pannier bags. (PHOTOS COURTESY L.L. BEAN, INC. AND SCHWINN SALES, INC.)

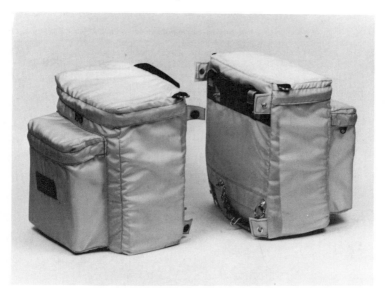

camping turns out to be the greatest fun you've ever had, the time will be ripe to look for a sleeping bag.

When you do begin shopping, you'll find that sleeping bags come in a variety of weights, determined by the amount of insulating material used. Of course, you need to select the lightest weight possible. Base your decision on the areas and seasons in which you'll be doing most of your traveling. For instance, suppose that you plan to camp only during the warmer times of the year and at lower altitudes. You're not going to need a bag with enough insulation to keep an arctic explorer or Everest climber warm. Rather, look for a bag that can handle nighttime temperature drops to 40 degrees Fahrenheit.

There's no mystery to finding such a bag. Usually, a commercially made bag is marked with its temperature rating. But don't depend on the rating alone. Also take into consideration the kind of person you are. Are you always shivering when everyone else is warm? Or are you the sort who goes about happily in short sleeves when your friends are bundling themselves up in fleece-lined coats or extra sweaters? Think about what you'll need for the most comfort at the least weight. Then talk with the sales clerk, who should be able to help you make the right selection.

So far as actual weight is concerned, you can find good quality bags that tip the scales at as little as a pound and a half. At maximum, your bag should weigh no more than three pounds.

Ground Cover

The ground cools at night. You can feel cold even in a good sleeping bag. You can give yourself some protection here by placing the bag on a ground cover. The cover will also help to keep the bag from getting dirty.

Many cyclists use their rain ponchos as ground covers. A better choice, however, is a sheet of light but durable plastic because you can spread it out farther beyond the borders of your sleeping bag. A sheet 4 × 8 feet or 8 × 10 feet will do fine, but I'd recommend the larger one. It will provide ample material that you can pull over the bag as a protection against the wet of an early morning dew or—if you're without a tent—a sudden shower in the night. Should rain strike as you're setting up camp, the cover can serve as a temporary shelter for your bike—or even for you.

You'll find that you can fold a sizable ground cover of lightweight plastic into a small, flat package for easy storage. The cost of the sheet is slight, only a few dollars.

Air Mattress

Some campers look on an air mattress as a luxury. They say that they can make a perfectly fine bed of pine needles or foilage for their sleeping bags. But most of my cycling friends feel that a mattress is a necessity. Their argument is that it takes quite a time to collect those pine needles. And, all too often, you have to search far and wide before finding enough.

I have to agree with my friends. Furthermore, the ground is hard, even with a cushion of pine needles. You need a good night's sleep to be ready for tomorrow's pedaling. The mattress can be a great help.

You must look carefully, though, when shopping for an air mattress. The standard types found in most stores are too heavy and bulky to store on the bike. Insist on a lightweight model that comes as close to one pound as you can get. And ask for one that's made of coated nylon. It's far more resistant to punctures than are the ordinary vinyl types.

One of the better mattresses around is made of several tough-skinned airtight tubes that can be inflated separately. With the individual tubes, there will be no air hiss when you turn over in your sleep. The tubes are easy to inflate and deflate. The mattress folds into a flat package for storage.

Another type features a series of replaceable vinyl tubes covered with fabric. It works well, but you must carry along a spare tube in case one is punctured.

If you feel that an air mattress is a bit too fancy or expensive, take a look at ground pads. They range in thickness from a quarter-inch to around two inches. Though usually bulkier than an air mattress, many can still be easily carried on a bike. You'll find them in camping and backpacking stores.

Tent

A tent is another item that can be called a luxury or a necessity. If you enjoy sleeping with nothing but the trees between you and the stars and if you don't mind huddling down inside your sleeping bag during a shower, then a tent is a luxury. But if you want some protection from the elements . . . well, you know the answer.

All sorts of tents are available on today's market. As usual, look for the lightweight one that folds into a compact bundle for storage. Stay away from the big fancy ones that weigh eight to ten pounds. The best ones for cyclists weight from three to five pounds.

As for the type of tent, a pup tent large enough for two campers will do fine; to save weight, pick one made of a durable plastic rather than a fabric. A tubular or triangular tent is another good possibility. It consists of three sides joined together and supported by a cord stretched between trees. Two of its sides angle downward and outward to form the walls. The third side extends from the base of one wall to the other and serves as a ground cover.

The pup tent is a shade more comfortable than its tubular relative. It has a wall at one end and entrance flaps at the other. The tubular tent is usually open at both ends, which means that you're going to have to put up with the wind blowing through.

If you don't want to buy a tent, you can easily make one of your own. Just get a piece of plastic large enough to give you and your tentmate sufficient width and headroom once you're inside. Then suspend it from a cord (try parachute cord about an eighth-inch thick) that you stretch between two trees. In case you can't find suitable trees, be sure to take along two collapsible support stakes. You also can run the support cord between your two bikes. Then anchor the edges of the walls in place, and you're in business.

Or you might try a plastic tarpaulin, which is nothing more than a large sheet punched with a number of grommets or festooned with a series of tie tapes. Thanks to the grommets and the tie tapes, the tarp can be fashioned into a variety of tent shapes. If you buy a tarp, be sure to invest in a nylon-coated one. Remember, it's far less vulnerable to punctures.

Punctures and tears are a problem for any plastic tent. They're bound to give you trouble at one time or another. So always treat the tent with special care. Since you're likely to go camping only a few times a year, your tent can last for quite a long while if you handle it carefully.

Stove

Here is yet another item that you may or may not regard as a necessity. Many campers prefer to forget about a stove and build campfires or take advantage of the stone fireplaces in public campgrounds. But today there is a growing tendency to regard a stove as essential for environmental and safety reasons.

The environmental reason? So many people are now visiting campgrounds that the normal supply of firewood is fast disappearing and campers are defacing the trees all around in their search for firewood. As for safety, many cyclists like to bed down in wooded areas other than campgrounds. It's fine to build a campfire in your own secluded spot, but there's always the danger of setting the surroundings aflame. The danger is greatly reduced when a stove is used. In fact, in many forested areas, open campfires are prohibited during the dry times of the year.

To avoid problems, you should look on the stove as an essential. It comes in a variety of models whose weight will serve the cyclist well. A top choice is the stove that is fueled by butane or propane capsules. It's light and compact. The capsules are easily handled; you simply open the valve and ignite the escaping gas with a match. And, since you're using a gas, there's no danger of the fuel spilling over your gear as you ride. The only disadvantage is that the capsules are more expensive than other types of fuel.

Another good choice is the stove powered by white gas. It is usually a little heavier than the butane or propane type but is still compact enough for easy storage. In their smaller models, both stoves can easily cook for one or two people. Some lightweight models, weighing as little as two pounds, can take care of four campers.

As always, search for the best you can get at the lightest weight. Avoid anything that looks big and threatens to rattle while you're riding. See if you can find something that weighs around two pounds.

If you're planning to do all your eating at restaurants, it will be a good idea to bring along a jellied fuel such as Sterno, which can be ignited right in its own can. It's nice to have around for heating soup or tea during a lunchtime break or a rest stop. Jellied fuels don't give off a particularly hot flame and so can be a bother for regular cooking.

Tote Bag

There's no question about this item being a necessity. Every camping party should have a tote bag for food storage at the campsite. It's a must if you're to keep your supplies out of the reach of such visitors as deer, raccoons, bears, and even ants. The bag should be suspended from a tree limb by means of a rope and should hang at least ten feet above the ground.

The bag can also be used for carrying food to the campsite from a nearby grocery store.

You can use practically any kind of bag that you wish. It may be made of fabric or a strong plastic. One of the best bags is the stretch net type, but a gunny sack will serve just as well. So will a duffle bag or pillow slip. Or a backpack.

Now that we've mentioned the backpack, let's talk some more about it. It's fine for storing your food at the campsite or for carrying a few supplies in from a nearby store. But, unlike the hiker, you should avoid it (or its cousin, the knapsack) as a general carrier for food or gear while you are riding. When loaded and strapped to your back, the pack bears down too heavily for easy pedaling and will tire you quickly. Furthermore, riding high on your back, it lifts the center of gravity and makes the bike unstable. Finally, it can interfere with those over-the-shoulder glances for cars coming up from the rear. So, unless you plan to use it for campsite storage or for short runs to the grocery store, you'd best leave your backpack at home.

And while we're on the subject of food, we should remember something that we said in Chapter 8. Because grocery stores seem to be just about everywhere, you won't need to carry much food on your bike unless you're really heading into the boondocks. Most public campgrounds have grocery stores near at hand, often no more than a half-hour ride away. You can either pick up all the necessary food just before you enter the grounds or cycle out for it at intervals during your stay. Of course, if you're going to be in a desolate area, make sure that you have sufficient rations and water. Remember that dehydrated rations are always an advantage for the cyclist because they weigh little and are compactly packaged.

Camp Light

Once again, we come to an item with a question mark—necessity or luxury?

Campers who light their own campfire are often content with its glow for nighttime illumination. But, unless you're happy to see your way about by moonlight, you'll want a lamp of some sort if you've decided that it's best not to have a campfire.

As is true of all camping gear, there are plenty of lamps to choose from. You can buy battery-powered lights that cast a brilliant beam. You can choose a lamp that's powered by butane. Or you can choose one of the primus types that burn white gas. Each light works well but also manages to have some disadvantages. The batteries used in most lights are heavy. The butane and primus lamps employ delicate mantles that can break easily, making it necessary for you to pack some substitutes.

And so only one piece of advice, really, can be given here. As you look for a lamp that is lightweight and compact, tell the sales clerk your needs and what you can afford to spend for a light. Explain your packing problems. He or she will then be able to help you find the lamp that will best serve you.

Incidentally, you might want to think about depending on candles instead of a lamp. So far as cost is concerned, they can't be beaten. They're to be found in grocery stores everywhere. In camp, you can stand them by themselves or place them in a small lantern.

And they're certainly far more camplike than a glaring battery light. Just be careful of accidental fires.

In addition to the personal touring gear mentioned in Chapter 8—your toiletries and such—you'll need to bring along some items meant especially for camping.

First, you'll need a pocketknife and a compass. Obviously, you'll find all sorts of uses for the pocketknife, everything from cleaning fish to opening food packages and cutting twigs for a campfire. The compass may turn out to be a vital help on a hike through the hills or a thick woods. Since some knives come with a compass in their handles, you may want to combine the two. When choosing a knife, try not to pick a bulky one. It can be a bother there in your pocket, rubbing against your skin as you hike or pedal.

Next, be sure to have a shovel and a hatchet, especially a shovel. You'll find that the U. S. Forest Service now requires all camping parties to have a shovel for fighting fires. The most easily packed shovel is the type with a folding handle. The hatchet blade should be sheathed so that it doesn't cut into your other gear as you ride—or into you as you unpack it. You can purchase a hatchet and shovel at a sporting goods shop or an army surplus store.

Now for your cooking and eating utensils. The number of cooking utensils needed will depend on the number of people camping with you. If you're alone or with a friend, you should do quite well with a nesting pot, a pan for frying, and a pot for coffee or tea. For a party of four, it will be a good idea to add another pot or pan. Each camper should have a metal plate, cup, knife, fork, and spoon. Cups can be made to do double duty for heating water or soup.

If you wish, you may carry an army mess kit that combines a pan, a plate, and eating utensils in a single package. You'll carry your cup and other pots separately, of course. If you plan to assemble the gear for your group, you might look at cooking kits. They usually come equipped with six plates and cups.

Aluminum is the best material for cooking and eating ware. It's tough and weighs next to nothing. Everything you'll need is now made of it. Avoid such "heavyweights" as cast iron frying pans. You may be tempted to use paper plates, but shy away from them. They're disposable, yes, and free you from the annoyance of washing up after a meal. But, since you'll have to carry a bundle of them to see you through, they're going to take up too much precious space in your pannier bags.

Round out your cooking gear with a spatula, a couple of tablespoons, two dish towels, a scrub pad, and two pot holders. It will also be a good idea to bring along a package of moist disposable towels so that you can wash your hands if they become sticky.

Should you forget the pot holders, you can use a pair of pliers from your repair kit to lift hot pots and pans.

And—oh, yes—don't forget to pack a couple of packages of matches. Keep them in a waterproof wrapping.

If you're out with a friend or a group, there's no need for every camper to carry all the personal items that we've mentioned. For instance, one or two hatchets and shovels may do for the entire party. The same goes for the compass and cooking utensils. Pick the number of items that you determine will see you through. Then, to conserve weight for each cyclist, distribute them among the campers for packing, letting one person carry the camp light, another the stove, and another the cooking utensils.

A SPECIAL PIECE OF EQUIPMENT

But let's say that you're traveling with a large group or with your family. There's the chance that, even with the gear kept at a minimum and distributed equally among the campers, you'll still have more than you can load aboard the bikes. For instance, when camping with the family, you may have a large tent that will hold all the sleepers. Or your mother or dad may be a gourmet cook who insists on taking along all the things that will enable you to dine out in style there under the trees.

So what to do? Obviously, for safety's sake, don't overload the bikes. Rather, it's time to talk about bringing a sag wagon along for all the gear. Or, if the idea of driving doesn't appeal to anyone, you can consider a special piece of equipment—a cargo trailer.

A cargo trailer is a two-wheel carrier that attaches to the rear of the bike. Depending on what you're taking, it may be able to handle all your gear or a major portion of it. But you must be certain to buy a trailer that's on the expensive side so that you'll be assured it will track well. A poorly made model that wobbles and sways can give you trouble and even cause a bad spill, especially on a downgrade.

And be particularly alert when towing the trailer. With its two wheels, it sticks out a fair distance to either side of the bike. On a narrow road with a broken shoulder, you really have to "thread the needle," keeping one wheel off the shoulder if possible and watching that the other doesn't jut out into the path of passing cars.

WHERE TO GO

If you're puzzled as to where to go camping, remember all those organizations, both local and national, that helped you with your regular tours. They can be as good at pointing out fine camping areas as they were at suggesting tour routes. Your city, county, and state park departments can be of particular help. The national park system has information on federal parks and camping facilities all across the country.

When planning to use a public campground or park, be sure to inquire ahead of time to see if there will be room for you. Summertime camping seems to be more popular than ever these days, and so you'll probably have to reserve a space for your party. An inquiry will also provide you with information about the entrance fee (it's usually a nominal one) and the camping regulations. You may inquire by calling or writing the park office or the agency in charge.

PICKING A CAMPSITE

At times, you'll be given a certain space in a campground. At other times, you'll be able to choose your own spot, just as you will when settling into some area other than a campground.

When choosing a campsite, always look for one where water is readily available. It's wisest to settle on a spot where the water is piped in. Your chances are then better that the water will be fit to drink. Especially in these days of widespread pollution, avoid taking your water directly from a lake or stream. And remember that even piped water in an outdoor area may not be up to standard. If you're even slightly in doubt about its quality, boil the water before you use it. You should also bring along some purification tablets for roadside drinks and soups when you don't have the time to build a fire or heat your stove for boiling. You can buy the tablets at any sporting goods store.

Try also to pick a spot that gets its fair share of both sun and shade. A campsite that's perennially in shade can be happily cool at first, but may prove too chilly or even depressing after several days. On the other hand, no one needs to explain how the sun can bake you if you're camped in an open field.

Finally, try to pick a spot that's sheltered from the wind. There's bound to be some wind, but it can make life miserable—particularly when you're trying to cook—if it comes whipping in all the while or for long stretches at a time. If you're bedding down in an open-ended tent, find the most protected area of the site for it. You might also pitch it so that the wind will strike it from the side rather than come blowing through.

As you know, you may set up your "home away from home" at any spot where camping is permitted. But please remember that word *permitted*. Never go where you're not wanted. Even in public parks, you'll find areas where camping is prohibited, perhaps because of the fire danger, perhaps to protect the ecology. A responsible camper always stays clear of them.

You must be quite as responsible when you camp somewhere other than a campground or park. Take care that you don't bed down on government or private land not open to visitors. You can glimpse numerous clues as to whether you're welcome or not. You may see the traces of earlier campsites. Look for signs that say camping is permitted. In particular, watch for "no trespassing" signs and never disobey them.

If you're passing through an area and are in doubt about where you can camp, stop at a nearby town or store and ask for advice. Should you eye a spot on private land, be sure to ask the owner's permission to stop there.

Of course, wherever you may be, take care to keep your campsite neat during your stay. Clean the spot thoroughly before leaving, removing every last scrap of paper. Don't be one of those litterbugs who seem to be doing all they can to destroy our country's beauty spots. Leave the campsite the way you would like to find it.

And need this be said? If you build a campfire, always make certain that it's completely out when you leave the campsite for a short while or for good.

CAMPING IS AN art. There's so much to learn about it, even though we've covered quite a bit of ground in this chapter. In your local library or bookstore, you'll find a great many books and guides that can help turn you into an expert camper. Why not take a few minutes to go "touring" for them? They're not only helpful but fun to read as well. In fact, on a stormy day that keeps you indoors, they're the next best thing to packing your bike and taking off.

CHAPTER 10

Taking Care of Your Bike

YOU'RE GOING TO be riding for many miles and steering your bike along all sorts of roads, from the very worst to the very best. Though its life is sure to be a rugged one, your bike is sturdy and will serve you well and faithfully. But it will do so only if you take proper care of it. You must always keep it in top condition and constantly watch for those ailments that, though they seem minor today, can turn into tomorrow's mighty headaches if left untended.

Of course, no matter how kindly and carefully you treat it, your bike is going to break down from time to time. All machines do, and a bicycle is no exception. Its gears can't help developing problems after so much shifting, nor can the tires keep from being punctured when you run over a nail or a jagged piece of glass. These are difficulties that every cyclist encounters sooner or later on the road, and you must know how to handle them so that you can get going again.

And so this chapter has two purposes: to explain some simple ways to keep your bike in good shape and to talk about the roadside repairs that you'll most likely be called on to make. We'll start with a few general tips. Then we'll look at the various parts of the bike.

MAINTENANCE AND REPAIR: THE BASIC RULES

Good bicycle maintenance and repair must begin with five basic rules.

First, always keep your bike clean. All roads are dusty. Dirt, grime, and road oil quickly gather and build up on moving parts. The bike becomes difficult to pedal. Worse yet, the grit works its way among the many bearings and wears them out, shortening their life spans by months or even years. Right from the start, develop the habit of cleaning the bike regularly and after any particularly dusty or oily ride.

But, except for the painted surfaces of the frame, never clean the bike with water. Rust is a constant threat. You should use a solvent instead. Kerosene works well, but you have to handle it with extra caution because it's highly flammable. Top choices for cleaning are Bullshot and WD-40; you will find both products at bicycle and auto shops.

Second, keep the bike well lubricated. Just what does "well lubricated" mean? There's no need to pour a can of oil on every joint and into every crevice. Too much oil can be harmful because it attracts and holds even more dirt and grime. A few drops of a light-weight oil applied to the moving parts on a regular basis will do the job. For instance, if you have coaster brakes, you'll find that the hub requires no more than a teaspoon of oil three or four times a year.

Third, be sure to give the bike a major lubrication once a year. At that time, take apart such components as the hubs, chainwheel axles, and steering head assemblies, clean them, and oil them. Worn parts should be replaced. If you're a mechanic and have the necessary tools, you can do the job yourself at home. Everyone else should head for the repairman at the bike shop. The work will cost a few dollars, but the comfort of knowing that things are being done by an expert will make the expense worthwhile.

Next, when traveling, always take along a good repair manual. Some repairs can be complex, and the details of repair can differ slightly among the various makes of bicycles. A manual that tells you what to do with your particular bike is invaluable. With the manual—plus your own good sense and perhaps the help of a friend—you'll have a good chance of successfully completing a roadside repair or at least bringing the bike to the point where you can ride it to the fix-it shop in the next town. The world is full of excellent manuals. One is waiting for you at your local bike shop.

Finally, a rule for the nonmechanics of this world. Some riders love to take their bikes apart and fix them. Others hate the idea because they don't know a screwdriver from a bolt. If you're among the latter, you still must teach yourself how to clean and oil the bike and how to make minor adjustments and repairs. They're simply handled and will save you much money, time, and frustration. Major repairs can be left to the bike shop. Just be sure not to let any threatening problem go ignored for long before taking the bike in.

Now let's turn to the various bike parts, starting with the all-important brakes.

BRAKES

As you know, your brakes will usually be the coaster or caliper type. If they're coasters, they'll need that teaspoon of oil three or four times a year. In addition, you should routinely check the bolt that holds the brake arm clamped to the chain stay. Make certain that it hasn't loosened during your travels. A few turns with a wrench will take care of things.

What if coasters give you trouble as you ride? Even if you're a pretty good mechanic, you'll be wise to turn the problem over to the bike shop. Special tools are required to take a coaster apart and repair it. Also, you'll probably find that the trouble is caused by worn interior parts. They'll need to be replaced.

Now for some caliper talk. The illustration shows two kinds of calipers: the side-pull and the center-pull. Each is activated by the cable that comes down from the brake lever. On the side-pull model (Picture A) the cable is linked to one side of the caliper arms. On the center-pull (B) it drops down in front of the head tube and connects to the center of a yoke rising out of the caliper arms. At one point on its

SIDE-PULL AND CENTER-PULL CALIPERS

way to the yoke, the cable is secured to the head tube by means of a clip with a bolt in it.

The two caliper systems suffer from the same malady. The cable stretches with use, interfering with the calipers' efficiency. This cable can, however, be adjusted easily to a shorter or longer length. The center-pull adjustment is made at the bolt on the clip that holds the cable to the head tube; a further adjustment can be made at the bolt connecting the cable to the yoke. On the side-pull, the adjustment is made at the two bolts that, as illustrated, are located one above the other.

When the brake cables are properly adjusted, the brake pads should hang about one-eighth to one-fourth inch out from the wheel rims when not in use. Spin the wheels to be sure that the rims do not touch the pads at any point. If you find that a brake cable is worn or frayed, clip a new one into its place.

The brake pads, as we mentioned, must come against the braking surface on the wheel rim when the levers are squeezed. The correct position is pictured. When they fail to hit right on target, you have one of two problems on your hands: either the pads have slipped a little, or they are worn and in need of replacement.

Both the replacement and an adjustment for slippage are easily made. You can see in the illustration that the pad and its metal holder are locked in place by means of a bolt that passes through a slot in the caliper arm. To adjust, loosen the bolt and move

BRAKE PAD ON BRAKING SURFACE

the pad and holder to the desired position. For replacement, loosen the bolt until the pad and holder come away.

You may use a new pad-and-holder unit as a replacement. Or you may insert a new pad into your present holder. A new unit is slightly more expensive, but its convenience makes the extra cost worthwhile. Inserting a new pad into a present holder can be a ticklish little job at times.

One caution: some holders keep the pad clamped in place with three walls—two that run lengthwise and a third that stretches across one end. The opposite end is left open for the insertion of new pads. When using a holder such as this, be sure to bolt it into place with the open end facing the *rear* of the bike. Otherwise, you'll risk having the pad fly out as you brake.

Check your wheels regularly to see that they're "true" —that is, free of wobble and hop. Wobble is a side-to-side movement. Hop is an up-and-down dance. Both cause rapid tire wear and reduce braking efficiency.

To check for trueness, have a friend hold the bike so that the wheel is a couple inches off the ground. Give the wheel a good flick and then watch closely as it spins. If it wobbles more than a sixteenth of an inch off center, you've got a problem. The same goes if it hops more than a sixteenth of an inch.

The job of truing a wheel can be a complex one and is best left to the bike shop. The shop has a special adjustment jig—not to mention an expert repairman—for the job.

There are times, though, when you may be able to take care of things yourself. Perhaps one or two loose spokes are causing the problem. Spin the wheel and lightly touch the passing spokes with a stick or pencil. Those that are tightly in place will give off a musical pinging sound. Determine the position of the off-key ones and tighten them with the spoke wrench from your tool kit. It's best to "snug" them tight. This means to take most of the looseness out of them at first and then go a quarter-turn at a time for the rest of the way, testing the wheel for trueness after each quarter-turn.

If the wheel continues to wobble after the tightening, you'll need to experiment a bit. Try loosening the problem spokes a trace; you may have tightened them too much. Spin the wheel to see the points where the wobble brings it against or close to the brake pads; then tighten the spokes on the side opposite that point. If the experiments fail, then it's time to hunt up the repairman.

A trueness problem can also be caused by worn bearings in the hub. Check to see that the hub is securely bolted in place. Off you go to the bike shop if it is. The bearings need to be replaced.

TIRE CHANGE

While we're on the subject of wheels, let's get to that most common of all roadside repairs—the flat tire.

First off, when a tire goes flat, don't immediately roll up your sleeves and remove the wheel. Instead, find out whether the leak is in the valve or the tube. Reinflate the tire and daub the mouth of the valve with water or saliva. If a bubble rises, the problem is a valve leak. Remove the valve core and take a look at the rubber at its base. If you find no cracks or dry spots there, replace the valve core and tighten it firmly. The core simply may have been loose or poorly seated because of dirt. Put some more moisture on the valve mouth. If no bubble rises, you can start pedaling again.

If there's no leak in the valve, then it's time to roll up your sleeves. Off must come the wheel so that you can take the tube out and patch it. Depending on the style of bike, wheels are removed by loosening either the axle nuts or the quick release mechanism. Before removal, the rear wheel must be shifted to a point where the chain comes free. If the bike has coaster brakes, you'll have to free the brake arm before removal. On three- and five-speed bikes, the shift cable must be unlinked. With a ten-speed, be sure that the chain is on the smallest, outer sprocket. For specific information on the design features in your bike that may affect wheel removal, check your manual.

Before freeing the wheel, you should take the valve core out of the tire so that the air can quickly escape. Once the wheel is off, press the remaining air out. Now you may be able to reach the tube by massaging the tire casing off the rim with your fingers. It's a job, though, that can require a great deal of strength, and so you'd best count on using tire irons, two of them.

Stand the wheel so that the valve is down at your feet. Pry the first iron between the tire casing and the rim up at the top. Work carefully so that the iron won't puncture or split the tube. When some of the casing comes out, hold the iron in place and slip the second iron into the gap, at a point about two or three inches away. When a further stretch of the casing has freed itself, place the first iron in the new gap and begin prying. Alternating the irons in this fashion, continue around the rim until one side of the casing is completely free.

Remove the tube, bringing the valve out last. Now the job of searching for the leak begins. Replace the valve core and inflate the tube. Turn the tube slowly in your hands as you look for the slightest split or puncture. If you see none, try listening for a hissing sound, holding the tube near your ear if need be. If there is a stream or pond nearby, immerse the tube in it and again watch for those telltale bubbles. If there's no stream, coat the tire with a film of water from your canteen.

One way or another, you'll find the leak—and usually without much fuss. Now patching can begin. First, thoroughly dry the area to be patched if you've wet it. Next, using the grater from your patch kit, roughen the surface around the leak, making certain that you cover an area larger than the patch you plan to use. Now coat the area with your rubber cement and stand by until it becomes tacky. You must also coat the patch with cement unless it comes prepared with stickum. When everything is appropriately tacky, press the patch into place on the tube and hold it tightly there while drying begins.

Before reinserting the tube, you should check the casing thoroughly for the villain that caused the flat and remove it. Look the outside over for signs of nailheads and the like. Probe inside with your fingers for the point of a nail or a piece of glass that might be sticking through. Work carefully here so that you don't nick your fingers. Also feel for an interior split or crease that might have been responsible. You can cement a patch to a split or crease so that you can ride for the rest of the day. But plan to buy a new tire when you arrive home.

When you're ready to reinsert the tube, put some air in it, just enough to keep it from creasing as you work. Stand the wheel so that the valve hole is at the top. Insert the tube, circle the rim with it, pass the valve through the hole, and work a small area of casing back onto the rim. Now turn the wheel valve down and urge the casing onto the rim at the opposite end. You may be able to get it into place with your fingers. More likely, thanks to the curve of the rim, you'll have to use a tire iron (careful please—it's discouraging to puncture the tube again along about now). With the iron, work the casing onto the rim a few inches at a time until you've circled the wheel. At certain points, you may find that there is too much pressure in the tube for easy handling; just take some air out. Once everything is back in place, reset the valve core and inflate the tire to its proper pressure.

As a tourer, you'll probably ride on inflated clincher-type tires. But you may be among the few who use the "sew-up"—the lightweight, slender tire favored by racers. If so, you should always carry a spare tube. Patching a sew-up can be a headachy job at the roadside because, among other things, it requires the use of extra thin patches. It's easier to put in a new tube and forget the patching until you get home.

You can help to protect yourself against flats in a number of ways. Watch, of course, for all road hazards that can damage a tire. Never heedlessly bang into a curb or try to fly over one. And keep your tires inflated to the pressure recommended by the manufacturer; most tires have the recommended pressure imprinted on their walls. Finally, take great care if you have to fill your tires from the air pump at a gas station. A gas station pump releases a jet blast and can cause the tire to explode. When using the pump, put the nozzle against the valve for just an instant as you release the air.

GEARS AND DERAILLEURS

It goes without saying that gears and derailleurs are pretty complex mechanisms. Take your bike to the repair shop whenever these systems start to give you trouble. Don't attempt to fool with them unless you're naturally talented as a mechanic. And, even then, be sure to have a good manual at hand during your first adventures in repair.

But even if you lack mechanical skill, you must be able to keep the gears and derailleurs clean. Located close to the ground as they are, they're particularly vulnerable to dirt and road oil. Also, the passing chain adds its own oil and grime to the mess. When cleaning, start with a fairly stiff-bristled quarter-inch paintbrush. Brush the dirt away on all moving parts in the front and rear derailleurs, on all outer surfaces of the rear derailleur pulleys, on the cables, and on the shift levers. Then spray them with a solvent. Finish off by wiping away the excess solvent and grime with a soft cloth. For best upkeep, you should do this job every two months.

Complex though the gears and derailleurs may be, one roadside repair is easily made. Perhaps the chain will slip off a sprocket as you ride. Or perhaps it will decide not to move into your highest or lowest gear. The cause of these problems: the rear derailleur is out of proper adjustment.

If you look at the pulley system on the rear derailleur, you'll see two adjustment screws. They're usually marked *L* for low and *H* for high. Now you must raise the bike and hold it so that you can crank the pedals by hand and shift the gear levers. Then turn the appropriate adjustment screw to the right or left until the chain is seated properly on the sprocket. There are two adjustment screws on the front derailleur for taking care of problems up at the chain-wheels.

CHAIN

The chain is made up of a series of rollers with little spaces in between to catch the sprocket teeth on the rear wheel and the chainwheel. If the chain is to work well as it propels the bike forward, the rollers must spin easily when passing the teeth. But, located down low as it is, the chain is as vulnerable to dirt as are the gears and derailleurs. Grime can quickly clog the rollers and slow or stop their spinning. Pedaling becomes a chore. The roller surfaces eventually wear away, causing the chain to sag and even break.

Your best protection against chain trouble on the road is to keep the chain always as clean as possible. For a routine cleaning, set the bike so that you can hand-crank the pedals. Spray a length of chain—say, six to eight inches—with a solvent and then wipe it with a soft cloth. Now advance the chain a few inches and again spray and wipe. Repeat the process until you've done the entire chain. Each length will be clean when it looks shiny and slightly oily.

Once the entire chain is clean, lightly spray it again. Don't wipe the solvent away this time, but let it remain for a few moments. Then lubricate the chain with a lightweight oil (try 20-weight). Wipe away the excess. The bike should now be allowed to stand for an hour or two while the remainder of the excess oil drips off.

When working with oil or grease, never let them touch and stain the rubber parts of the bike. While the chain is dripping, it's wise to set the bike at an angle so that the oil will drop clear of the rear wheel.

Many cyclists do not like to use oil for chain maintenance, saying that it attracts too much dirt. They prefer a graphite lubricant instead.

Let's say that your chain is especially dirty. You may then need to remove it from the bike and soak it in kerosene. You can help matters along here by working the excess grime off with your fingers or a toothbrush during the soaking. At the end of the "bath," you may lubricate with graphite or a lightweight oil either before or after returning the chain to the bike.

How do you remove the chain for cleaning? If you own a coaster bike, you must open what is called the "master link." This link is easily recognized because it is equipped with special plates along its sides. Gently pry the plates off with a screwdriver, and the chain will divide itself. Return the chain to the bicycle by snapping the plates back in place.

A ten-speed chain does not have a master link. Instead, you must use a special rivet tool to open any of the links. Each roller is joined to its connecting plates by a tiny rivet. The tool punches the rivet inward so that the roller comes free and the link opens.

As we said in Chapter 8, you should carry an extra length of chain when you're on the road. A length of about six links will usually take care of a breakage problem. The rivet tool is used to remove the old links and install the new ones.

The pedals are so sturdy looking that they risk being ignored for long periods. But they, too, are positioned down low and need constant attention.

A pedal should spin freely at all times and so must be kept free of clogging dirt. To ensure a good spin, clean and oil all moving parts regularly. Start by brushing the grime from the spindle and follow with a solvent and wiping. Finish by applying a light-weight oil.

Dirt, however, isn't the only thing that will cause a pedal to stiffen on you. The spindle may be in need of adjustment. Remove the dust cap from the outer

PEDAL LUBRICATION

end of the spindle. Behind it, you'll find a lockwasher (Figure A), a locknut (Figure B), and, directly in front of the bearings, a cone nut (Figure C). Loosen the locknut and then adjust the cone nut until the pedal spins smoothly and easily.

You must also keep a constant eye on the point where the pedal joins the crank arm. The pedal is threaded into the arm and can unscrew itself somewhat as you ride. It then rocks up and down (sometimes so slightly that you won't feel the motion) and eventually strips its own threads and those in the arm. If you don't keep the pedal screwed tightly in place, you'll soon need a new one and a new crank arm. The cost can bite.

You can avoid all the fuss if you'll regularly take hold of the pedals and rock them up and down to see

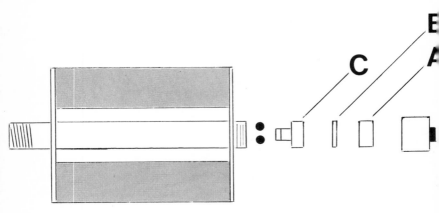

SPINDLE PARTS

if they're loose. You'll be surprised at the money you save.

AND THAT SEEMS to be just about all that I can say. Just let me add one more thing: wherever you pedal —whether close to home or far away—have a great trip.

Index

ABOUT THE AUTHOR

EDWARD F. DOLAN, JR. has written more than fifty books for young people and adults. A fourth-generation Californian, he was born in the San Francisco area and was raised in Los Angeles.

After serving with the 101st Airborne Division in World War II, Mr. Dolan wrote for radio and television. He then worked for a number of years as a newspaper reporter and a magazine editor.

In addition to his books, Mr. Dolan has written numerous magazine articles and stories.

All his books are nonfiction and cover such topics as sports, history, current events, and science and medicine. They include *Starting Soccer, The Complete Beginner's Guide to Gymnastics,* and *It Sounds like Fun: How to Use and Enjoy Your Tape Recorder and Stereo.*

Mr. Dolan and his wife Rose live in northern California. They have two grown children.